SAY
THIS
NOT
THAT

SAY THIS NOT THAT

HOW TO MASTER
7 DREADED CONVERSATIONS
AS A LEADER
IN THE MODERN WORKPLACE

CHRIS FLICKINGER

SAY THIS NOT THAT Copyright © 2020 by Christopher Flickinger.

All rights reserved. Printed in the United States of America. No part of this book my be used or reproduced in any manner whatsoever without written permission except in the case of brief quotations embodied in critical articles and reviews.

FIRST EDITION

ISBN 978-1-7326455-8-5

Design by Stephen Knezovich

To my brother Jonathan—a highly recognized and awarded executive HR leader—who has since passed on to be with the Lord. Shortly before he was tragically taken in a car wreck, he wrote me a note that is now framed in my office. It reads,

Be confident that you can help people develop both personally and professionally. At the end of the day, it's about people—the only asset a company truly has that appreciates in value.

I love you, Jonathan.

CONTENTS

INTRODUCTION
THE OBJECTIVE ... ix

PART 1 :: PERFORMANCE MINDSET
READING PEOPLE, PRODUCING RESULTS ... 3
PERFORMANCE **DISC**OVERY ... 9
WHAT'S WRONG WITH THAT PERSON? ... 15

PART 2 :: THE 7 DREADED CONVERSATIONS
1/ SOMEBODY MESSED UP. HOW DO I TELL THEM? ... 23
2/ SOMEONE ASKED ME FOR A RAISE. HOW DO I TURN THEM DOWN? ... 43
3/ SOMEONE HAS LOST THEIR MOJO. HOW DO I MOTIVATE THEM? ... 61
4/ SOMEONE EMBARRASSED THEMSELVES (OR THE COMPANY). HOW DO I MAKE SURE THEY NEVER DO IT AGAIN? ... 77
5/ I DON'T GET ALONG WITH THIS PERSON. HOW DO I LEAD THEM? ... 93
6/ SOMEONE WANTS TO PURSUE A REALLY BAD IDEA. HOW DO I CHANGE THEIR MIND? ... 107
7/ I HAVE TO DELIVER BAD NEWS. HOW DO I DO IT? ... 121

PART 3 :: BONUS CHAPTER
BETTER THAN GREAT ... 141
WHAT'S NEXT? ... 147

INTRODUCTION

THE OBJECTIVE

To Conduct More Effective Conversations

Welcome to a book about everyone's absolute favorite subject: difficult and uncomfortable conversations at work. If you're a manager, executive, or leader of any stripe, you simply can't avoid these tough talks. And, yes, they are tough talks—that's why so many us struggle with them. The truth is that too many of us dread these encounters, and the trouble is that now they're a big part of the job you've been tasked to navigate and resolve. So, how will you handle these Dreaded Conversations when they inevitably come up?

Your success in these conversations hinges on two factors. And yes, two out of two are required here. If you only check off *one*, then you might as well just do *none*.

Here's the first one: your part in these conversations has to inspire productivity. In other words, what you say during the conversation must generate *results* after it's over. In this case, "results" means productivity and profitability. The leaders I've worked with over the years don't get to stay in their positions for very long if productivity and profitability start slipping.

Here's the second one: your part in these conversations must contribute to a positive culture. If your culture is upbeat, welcoming, and helpful, then, as forty years of research shows, your employees will work smarter, longer, and more effectively than they would in a place with poor culture.

So with those two key factors in mind, what's the most effective way for leaders to communicate during one of these Dreaded Conversations? What do you say when you have to correct someone's mistake; when you need to motivate a lagging employee; when someone did something to embarrass the company; when you have to fire someone; when you have to dissuade someone from making a poor decision; or when you…

Well, you get the picture. At some point or another, every leader encounters these kinds of conversations. But no matter how often you deal with them, the element most critical to your success is *how* you communicate.

EXPERIENCE

As a performance consultant, I spend quite a bit of my time helping leaders prepare for and then engage in difficult conversations like these. Based on hundreds (maybe thousands) of encounters with my clients—everyone from senior-level executives to professional athletes, and from corner-store shops to billion-dollar conglomerates—I have discerned 7 common situations that produce difficulty (and dread) for most managers and executives.

The reasons they dread these conversations can vary widely, but "dread" is the common thread. Perhaps they feel dread because the conversation is extremely awkward or highly contentious. Maybe they don't want to impede productivity or foster animosity. Regardless, CEOs always share the same war stories with me: they tried this or that approach, and it just didn't work. In fact, their efforts caused an extremely negative impact on morale, performance, teamwork, culture, or output.

OBJECTIVE OUTCOME

That, in a nutshell, is the impetus for this book. We're going to examine seven of the most dreaded leadership conversations, identify the strategies that work and the strategies that don't, and then leave you with a series of (easy-to-use) scientific and psychological tools that will help make *any* conversation less difficult, much more productive, and extremely effective. By the end of this book, you will have everything you need to quit worrying about these Dreaded Conversations and start engaging with leadership communication that inspires productivity and a positive culture.

The tactics and strategies I'm about to share with you are not the normal, everyday communication and leadership tips you might read about in other business books. Rather, what you're about to encounter is a *proven* leadership communication system that I share with my clients to help them get further, faster, and be more effective within their teams and business.

The lessons in the pages to come are intended for high-performance individuals within business settings—the leaders, the managers, and the executives who need to see action, get results, and make money; the men and women who know their crafts and excel at their jobs but are challenged by working with certain people they find frustrating.

WEAPONS-GRADE STRATEGIES

The advanced tools and science behind this book's approach to resolving dreaded conversations is very similar in thinking to a particular strategy used in another highly tense situation. I come from a family with a long and decorated history of protecting the freedoms of the United States. At our family's Christmas dinner, every branch of the Armed Services is represented. Even the Special Forces has a seat at our table. So, while it may be common knowledge within my family, it may be news to you that our military utilizes two types of bombing strategies to either neutralize or advance on opposition forces

One type is often referred to as "carpet bombing." This strategy drops a large swath of bombs over the target in the hopes that at least one of them will successfully hit the mark. Think about any World War II movie you've seen where an Allied plane flies over German-occupied territory and drops dozens of bombs over the intended target. This strategy can be effective in certain situations, but it does have considerable drawbacks: it's expensive (because you have to use so many bombs), inefficient (the bomb-to-target strike ratio is low), and it greatly increases the risk of collateral damage (when you drop a huge number of bombs, you inevitably hit unintended targets).

Too often, the way leaders communicate with their employees and peers looks like carpet bombing. They know that something needs to be said and done. They have a general idea of the impact and outcome they want. But they generalize the way they engage with the conversation. In other words, they broad-brush their approach even though they know that people and personalities are extremely diverse. So, just like carpet bombing, the communication winds up inefficient, with lots of collateral damage, missed messages, unintended meanings, agitations, decreases in productivity, and detriments to the culture.

The second type of bombing strategy the military uses is called "precision guided." A bomb or missile is laser-guided to its target with extreme precision, efficiency, and impact. A very specific weapon hits a very specific target based on precise measurements and the surrounding conditions.

Similar to the advances in military technology, strategies for leadership communication have gotten quite a bit more precise too! Through the use of a unique science and proven psychological tools, you no longer have to guess how a coworker or teammate is hardwired to think, work, and act. In this book, I'm going to show you how to identify specific "Performance Profiles" within the people you see and work with every day. Additionally, I'm going to give you details on critical "adaptation" techniques for improving their performance (and subsequently, the *organization's* performance). In essence, you'll be able to laser-guide a specific message to a specific person based on surrounding conditions with extreme precision, efficiency, and impact.

SPECIFICALLY, YOU'LL KNOW HOW TO:

- Appeal to and speak to each profile
- Motivate the members of each profile
- Provide what a specific profile needs to know and hear
- Set and manage the right expectations with a specific profile
- Make your point in a way that resonates with a certain profile
- Avoid the words and approaches that do not resonate with certain profiles
- Arrive at agreement more quickly
- Reduce the amount of time it takes to address and resolve issues
- Say what you have to say to whom, how, and when
- Influence people and steer outcomes
- Correctly anticipate both the reception and the reaction of the people you manage
- Invigorate people to succeed
- Better evaluate the effectiveness of conversations with people of each profile
- Drive more productivity by using Chris' tried and true Performance Principles
- Foster a better corporate culture with more tactical communication

We're going to take the guesswork out of leading and connecting with other people and show you how to get more effective results. In business terms, this means you will get *further, faster, and be more effective as a leader!*

PART 1
PERFORMANCE MINDSET

CHAPTER 1

READING PEOPLE, PRODUCING RESULTS

What I'm about to share isn't meant to impress you, but rather, to impress *upon* you the impact that the material in this book can have on your leadership skills. So here it goes: I am one of world's top experts in workplace behavior analysis and personality profiles. You and I have never met, but if we do ever meet, then within a few minutes, I'll know a whole lot about how you lead, communicate, deal with conflict, and work within a team. I'll gather this information based on how you look, dress, and talk, where and how you position yourself relative to me, and what sorts of tics you have or gestures you make. If we don't meet face to face, I can gather many of the same conclusions about your personality based on the e-mails you send me or voice messages you leave on my phone. Ditto if you've created a Facebook or LinkedIn profile.

It gets even better! Based on these brief touchpoints, I'll know how you want to be talked to, the way you process information, which ideas will tickle your ears, and which ideas will immediately turn you off. I'll know what specifically causes you stress and irritation, how quickly you'll respond to my message, and whether I'm going to need to keep after you a little to ensure that progress gets made and you don't soon become distracted.

Yes, I can learn all of that just by being more keenly aware of some specific observations I can make about you. And this isn't some sort of new-age mysticism where I'm tuned in to the vibrations of your chakras either. My methods are steeped in proven science and psychological principles, but what has brought me success is the practical use of these tactics and strategies in real business settings. From these observations, I can quickly adapt my message, my approach, my positioning, my style, my words, and even my timing to ensure that you'll more easily connect to, receive, and be in agreement with what I have to say. In essence, based on my observations *about* you, I can fine-tune my message to specifically resonate *with* you.

Sounds a little like a superpower, right? This is among the reasons clients hire me. They soon master these "superpowers" too and become much more effective at working with the people they lead. This is what I will share with you in the chapters to come.

PROVE IT

Okay, so let me back up my claim of being one of the world's top experts. While I was working as a business consultant in my mid-twenties, multiple people (perhaps serendipitously) introduced me to a unique form of industrial psychology. The unique behavioral business science was called DISC, and I became fascinated by this long-established psychological tool. Actually, that's an understatement; I ate it up, not overlooking a single crumb. Then I took it a step further; I started adapting it and grafting it into my own art form, to the point that it *utterly transformed* my career.

I went from an average consultant and producer to becoming internationally recognized among the top 1% of performance consultants working within a global organization—year after year. I was also ranked among the top ten managers across the organization's worldwide footprint. My numbers and impact grew at unprecedented levels, and so did my business acumen. I was credited with revolutionizing my employer's hundred-year-old approach to the marketplace by successfully and *consistently* shifting its revenue model from preformatted public training classes to customized, private talent development sessions inside corporate enterprises.

My success kept growing, and so did my career, as I eventually opened a highly specialized consulting firm called *Performance Mindset and Development*. Today, we work with Fortune 500 companies, professional athletes, family-owned businesses, and mid-sized companies. Since I grew up in what's affectionately known as Steelers' Country, I naturally based the firm in Pittsburgh, PA. Our impressive reputation for improving performance soon grew. In fact, a client of ours, one of Pittsburgh's most recognizable companies, has tripled its revenue and increased its size by 40% since we began working with them. The president of this organization is on record giving much of the credit to us and our ability to catapult his firm forward.

The science and psychological tools I share within this book can be used to produce incredible results for individuals, teams, and businesses alike. And they will work for you as they have with so many of my clients.

ISN'T THERE AN APP FOR THIS?

Okay, hold on. I told you that DISC is a long-established psychological tool—not my own original concept. So can't you just take a test or assessment online to figure out the same information I'm about share with you? Yes and no. The cost for a DISC assessment ranges from free to hundreds of dollars. But the real catch has less to do with price than it does with *practicality*. Tomorrow, when you meet someone for the first time (a new client, a new hire, a potential investor) go ahead and ask them at the outset of your conversation to complete a DISC assessment for you. Let them know it will only take ten or fifteen minutes. Oh, and be sure to tell them how much more effective it will make the encounter.

Come on! No one is going to oblige such a request, no matter how much better it would make the situation. Even if there was an app on your phone with a mobile DISC assessment, who in the world has the time or the inclination to take it?

A more business-savvy strategy would be to know how to "read" people and their performance profiles. If you know the profiles, then you can better understand how someone's mind works, what this person needs and wants, what to avoid, and how to work more effectively with him or her. You would know if being more assertive would help or hurt your cause; if being highly detailed would score points with this person; or if citing your newest product would actually be a major deterrent to moving forward. Actually, you would know a lot of things about this person that could increase your chances of winning them over.

This book will show you how do all of that. Now, I can't promise mastery of the DISC model, as it has taken me years of experience to get there myself. But you definitely don't need a degree for this either, and you don't need mastery to make it work effectively for you. You just need to be willing and able to observe people's behaviors, categorize them within a proven scientific model, and then easily adapt your approach to connect to their personality. If you have a pair of eyes, a desire to improve, and this book at the ready, then you, my friend, will be good to go.

EXPERIENCED THEORY

The success I've realized from this DISC model isn't based merely on theories and concepts; it comes from firsthand experience, from work in the trenches, and from enduring challenges and driving business results. It's also rooted in important lessons I've learned along the way (mostly from my mistakes). In other words, these lessons will help you get ahead of the curve.

The best part is that if I can do this, and if my clients can do this, you can do this too. And if you're a manager or executive, this model will absolutely change the game for how you manage your people and get results. So let's start this journey. Let's get further, faster, and be more effective at managing difficult conversations and leading organizations that win!

RAISE THE RED FLAG!

You're thinking, *Wait a minute...It sounds like you're trying to teach me how to manipulate people.* That's an excellent observation, but it's not entirely accurate. What I'm suggesting isn't that you should do whatever you can to be disingenuous. We're not trying to figure out how to just *win* for the sake of advancing an agenda. Instead, I'm suggesting that if you can learn someone's performance profile—or, put another way, how they're prewired to view communication, teamwork, leadership, conflict, and a host of other items—then you can do a better job of talking to them, interacting with them, appealing to them, leading them, and influencing them. We're not trying to lie or manipulate so we can get what we want; we're trying to figure out how to speak at another person's level so that we can better understand each other—and ultimately, achieve the desired outcome more quickly and more effectively.

If that doesn't lower the red flag for you, consider this: you already do this all the time. Do you talk to your employee the same way you talk to your best friend? Do you talk to your partner at work the same way you talk to your partner in life? Do you talk to a child the same way you talk to an adult? The answer to all those questions (I hope) is "no." It's certainly a "no" for me, and it's a "no" on a really granular level. I don't just talk differently to all those people; I talk differently to individual people that fall into each of those categories. And it's only natural.

Think about children—yours or someone else's. The way you speak to a thirteen-year-old sounds different from the way you speak to a five-year-old and the way you speak to a three-year-old. The thirteen-year-old probably wouldn't respond well if you asked her in public if she had to use the potty. Likewise, the three-year-old isn't interested in your grasp of advanced baseball statistics. The way you answer their questions differs from age to age too. As the father of three highly inquisitive boys, I can tell you this is how it works! Even my twin boys take in and process my messages differently. The rules for the house are the same, but my wife and I have to shape and adapt our messages to each of them differently.

Even if you don't realize it, you already change the way you speak and interact with people all the time. You adjust yourself to suit your audience. The model we're going to be covering in the chapters to come just shows you how to do that more scientifically, and above all, more *effectively*.

OH, I LIKE THIS GAME

What we're talking about here is a game you've probably been playing for years: people watching. Except now we're going to learn how to play it at an advanced level, using science to give you a significant performance edge when interacting with others.

Now, if you're thinking, *This seems too difficult or too subjective*, don't worry. When I was first introduced to this, I had the same thought. Here's the thing: while it's true that I used this tool to help grow my reputation as one of the top performance consultants in the world, I'm not some unique blade of grass. I learned it, owned it, and made it work for me. Actually, I know you'll *get it* because the business leaders to whom I teach this skill *get it*, use it, and are dramatically more effective because of it and they see results. And in the end, not only will you be able to read people at an advanced level, you'll know exactly how to craft your message around what a specific colleague or employee will respond to best. And frankly, that's the true goal here—not just learning this unique science but using it to make these seven dreaded leadership conversations so much more effective and performance driven.

CHAPTER 2

PERFORMANCE DISCOVERY

Okay, so what does the DISC model look like? I'm glad you asked. You should know that there are slight variations between DISC models you may encounter on the Internet or between assessment firms. What I'm about to share with you is a composite of many of these models (including that special, personalized twist I told you about earlier) and *not* just theories out of a book. Instead, you're about to see years' worth of real, in-the-trenches, practical experience using DISC across thousands of people and hundreds of companies. The descriptions, nuances, and conversation structures I'm about to detail among the profiles are not only tried and true, but they have allowed me to bring tremendous performance improvement to my clients.

THE LONG AND SHORT OF THE SCIENCE

As we go through this process of examining the seven most dreaded leadership conversations, you're going to get really familiar with these four letters: D-I-S-C. Maybe you've seen them before you even picked up this book. This science can be traced back to the ancient Greeks and then through the millennia to present day in a variety of forms. It really started to take shape in the early 1900s, when a very intelligent man of eclectic talents, William Marston, fashioned what is known today as DISC.

Marston's life is a fascinating study. He earned three degrees from Harvard University, was a published author in some of the most prestigious psychological journals in the country and served as a featured lecturer of psychology at some of the world's finest schools. He's probably best known as the inventor of the lie detector test used by crime fighting agencies across the world. And for the crescendo, he was also the creator of one of the most recognizable comic book characters in history: Wonder Woman. I told you he was a man of eclectic talents!

Each letter in the DISC model stands for a unique psychological profile—a certain way of thinking, working, and approaching the business world. Each person's personality is made up of a mixture of all four letters at varying levels. As for the letters themselves, each stands for its own unique profile: Driver, Influencer, Stabilizer, and Conscientious. Quick note: I've also seen some variations on these names (such as "Compliant" for C), but no matter what names are used, the letters still represent the same psychological profiles across the board.

D	**I**	**S**	**C**
DRIVER	INFLUENCER	STABILIZER	CONSCIENTIOUS
(Extrovert—Aggressive)	*(Extrovert-Friendly)*	*(Introvert-Polite)*	*(Introvert-Critical)*

Each profile resides on a spectrum from 0 to 10, and everyone falls somewhere inside the spectrum. Most commonly, people are going to display and use the traits of just two letters. We would say these letters are dominant when they score a 5 or above on the spectrum.

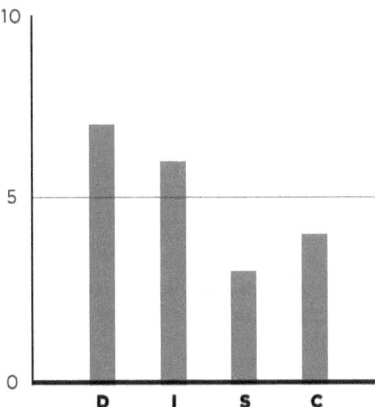

For example, your "D" and "C" letters might be higher (dominant) on the scale than your coworker's, while your "I" and "S" letters might be lower (recessive) on the scale. There's no right or wrong number to achieve here. No profile is good or bad, smart or dumb. The profiles just are what they are. Each has its strengths and corresponding blind spots. So don't stress about wanting to be a certain profile. They are all very much needed, especially when people are working in a team.

So, from now on, when you encounter someone—Ian in accounting, Christie in operations—try to look for which two profile letters they use to do their jobs.

One quick, last note: you can expect a person's two dominant letters to remain consistent at work. It's not like Ian will naturally be one set of letters on Monday and Tuesday but by the end of the week, he's the opposite two letters. It doesn't work like this. Ian's two dominant letters on Monday will be his same two dominant letters next Friday, next month, and next year.

On the next page, you will find it in (okay, slightly larger than) bite-sized form. Keep in mind that this isn't an exhaustive list, but it *will* begin opening your eyes to a new, unique world of people science.

PERFORMANCE DISCOVERY

D DRIVER	**I** INFLUENCER	**S** STABILIZER	**C** CONSCIENTIOUS
OBSERVABLE INDICATORS	OBSERVABLE INDICATORS	OBSERVABLE INDICATORS	OBSERVABLE INDICATORS
APPEARANCE - Very practical - Dresses quickly	**APPEARANCE** - Flash & sizzle - High maintenance	**APPEARANCE** - Neat & organized - Traditional - Professional	**APPEARANCE** - Thinking, analyzing - Skeptical - Nerdy, geeky
EMAIL/VOICEMAIL RESPONSES - Brief (few words) - Focuses on ROI & fast results	**EMAIL/VOICEMAIL RESPONSES** - Longer (stories) - Clever e-signature - Uses "I" a lot	**EMAIL/VOICEMAIL RESPONSES** - Paragraphs (long) - Explains process, recalls the history - Asks for more information - Uses standard company away message	**EMAIL/VOICEMAIL RESPONSES** - Cites specific, technical points - Asks questions (in critical tone) - Expresses doubt - Copies everyone
BODY LANGUAGE - Nervous energy - Ansty - Leans forward - Aggressive - Confident	**BODY LANGUAGE** - Touches others - Smiles a lot - Highly animated - Shows emotion - Disorganized	**BODY LANGUAGE** - Cautious, deliberate - Shows little emotion - Listens intently - Takes lots of notes	**BODY LANGUAGE** - Don't touch me - Thinking, analyzing - Moody - Arms crossed, head tilted
SPEECH - Loud & forceful - Direct & blunt - Crass, rough & curt Interrupts others	**SPEECH** - Long-winded - Tells stories, jokes - Character voices - Optimistic	**SPEECH** - Soft spoken - Slow to speak up - Process oriented - Shows concern for others - Loyalty, tradition	**SPEECH** - Questions everything - Cites rules, details & technical points - Pessimistic & critical - Logical, reasoned
VIBE - Conquer, achieve - Go get results - Quick decisions	**VIBE** - Fun and exciting - Center of attention	**VIBE** - Slow paced - Information gatherer	**VIBE** - Very smart - Detailed - Condescending
D DRIVER	**I** INFLUENCER	**S** STABILIZER	**C** CONSCIENTIOUS
(Extrovert-Aggressive)	*(Extrovert-Friendly)*	*(Introvert-Polite)*	*(Introvert-Critical)*

Here's a guess: You're looking at that list and going, "Whoa, whoa, whoa. I thought he said this wasn't complicated." I get it; that's a lot to absorb in one glance. But trust me, this is a simple breakdown of the system.

Okay, let me make it even easier with a little trick I show my clients. You don't have to remember all of the fancy terms, descriptors, and traits; you just have to remember a single person who portrays a specific letter at an extremely high level. In other words, rather than remembering a list of factors on a graph (which few people could do easily), it's much easier to find a person who embodies the extreme traits of each letter and then compare everyone you meet to that representative person. It's even better if these "example-people" are from your own life.

For instance, my father is my representative "High-D" (the Driver). He would be a 10 on the D scale. I may not be able to recall the full list of factors of the D profile, but I can certainly recall my dad's traits and compare them to each person I meet. I'll ask myself, "Does this person demonstrate a lot of characteristics similar to Dad's? Some? Or very few?" I can do this same thing with my representative High-I, representative High-S, and representative High-C. By comparing and contrasting the people I meet with my representatives, I can arrive at a reasonable (and quick) approximation of their unique performance profile.

Can't think of anyone from your own life? Then perhaps a few celebrities might help. Here are a few that my clients have often used to represent the profiles:

D
President Donald Trump
Judge Judy
Captain James T. Kirk (*Star Trek*)

I
President Bill Clinton
Kevin Hart
Scotty (*Star Trek*)

S
President Jimmy Carter
Mother Teresa
Dr. "Bones" McCoy (*Star Trek*)

C
Head Coach Bill Belichick
Bill Gates
Mr. Spock (*Star Trek*)

Here's a good tip: whenever you meet someone new, just identify which one or two letters are the most dominant in their profile. You don't have to codify each profile letter exactly on the spectrum before you can effectively engage with the person. Just look for the person's most glaringly dominant one or two profile letters.

That level of detail is all that's required for you to be highly effective using DISC. Remember, the DISC mastery reputation I developed was *not* based on giving people tests and drilling down into the granular specifics of their performance profiles. Rather, it was based on learning *how to read and adapt* to people on the spot. So, if you can just determine a person's most dominant profile letter (or two), and then adapt yourself to that profile, you will get further, faster, and be tremendously more effective with others.

CHAPTER 3

WHAT'S WRONG WITH THIS PERSON?

If you've held a management or executive position for any amount of time, you've probably noticed that what works for some people doesn't work for others. How often have you prepared and delivered a well-reasoned, thought-out, articulate message, only for a colleague, employee, or client to not "get it," disagree with you, or even show resistance?

Similarly, we often question people's actions and then assign motives, character labels, and accusations.

"Why did he do that?"
"Why would she say that?"
"He never follows through."
"She's always distracted."
"He takes forever."
"She's too sensitive."
"He's such a jerk."
"She's a total witch."
"He only cares about the price."
"She can't make a decision."
"He doesn't seem to trust us."

More often than not, none of those things are accurate (although I have to admit that sometimes they're spot on). It's much more likely that you just didn't deliver the message in a way that appealed to the recipient. But that's one of the secrets of good business; you have to be able to connect and resonate with others in ways that appeal to them.

Yet, I've encountered leaders from the executive suite to the frontline who share messages with their employees, and sometimes even with their customers, based on how that leader would want to hear it rather than how the audience would best digest and be enticed by it. This is a big problem!

If they understood the DISC profiles, then these leaders could deliver a laser-guided message that keeps the employee's attention, resonates deep within the psyche, and moves the person to take action that's in their profile's best interest.

This is particularly true in sales. Often, sales forces will spend countless hours trying to develop *the* perfect pitch to attract customers; but there's no such thing as *the* perfect pitch that will connect with *every* customer, because customers are all so different. Instead, when a sales manager brings me in, I'll help the team develop a handful of specific pitches that they can then easily insert into conversations with specific clients and prospects based on the unique personalities they've observed. The impact is immediate. It's a huge part of why these lessons have given me a performance edge, and it's exactly why they'll give you a performance edge too.

So, what type of laser-guided message and approach zeroes in on each specific profile? Here's a snapshot of the science:

D DRIVER	**I** INFLUENCER	**S** STABILIZER	**C** CONSCIENTIOUS
OBSERVABLE INDICATORS	OBSERVABLE INDICATORS	OBSERVABLE INDICATORS	OBSERVABLE INDICATORS
COMMUNICATING WITH A HIGH D	**COMMUNICATING WITH A HIGH I**	**COMMUNICATING WITH A HIGH S**	**COMMUNICATING WITH A HIGH C**
• Respect their time • Tell them exactly how long this will take • Talk in terms of the results and ROI • Keep it simple • Be down to earth and real • Be clear, specific, brief, and to the point • Stick to business • *Don't* give too many details • *Don't* include stories • *Don't* appear disorganized • *Don't* discuss the process	• Recognize their strengths • Be fun and exciting • Make them the hero • Allow them time to talk • Be optimistic • Talk in terms of their personal interests • Sell ideas and concepts through stories • Sell on their emotion, image, status, and likeability • *Don't* embarrass them • *Don't* control the conversation • *Don't* use only logic • *Don't* be cold, unfriendly	• Ask them about others, especially family and friends • Lay out sequence, plan, or list • Show that your case has been thought out, time tested, or traditional • Present your case softly, non-threatening • Ask "how?" questions to draw their opinion • Help them prioritize • *Don't* pressure for a quick decision • *Don't* yell at them • *Don't* supervise them • *Don't* be insensitive	• Prepare your "case" in advance • Stick to business • Be accurate, realistic, and detailed • Go beyond expectations • Provide third-party proof • Ask them questions to draw out their thoughts • Focus on quality and compliance Allow for private time to think • *Don't* be too emotional • *Don't* say, "you're wrong" • *Don't* use propaganda • *Don't* appear "salesy" • *Don't* pressure for a quick decision
(Extrovert-Aggressive)	*(Extrovert-Friendly)*	*(Introvert-Polite)*	*(Introvert-Critical)*

THE STRUCTURE

Now that you have the basics of DISC, it's time to focus and apply its proven science to leadership—specifically, to those 7 Dreaded Conversations. I'm going to show you how to analyze each situation and identify the profiles involved, and then I will present you with strategies to resolve the problems these conversations often create.

Each chapter to come will feature this same structure:

THE CONVERSATION

After identifying the problem that we need to resolve with this Dreaded Conversation, I will create two fictional characters who will then act out a common example of how the conversation might progress in the real world.

In fact, it will be *very* real. I've coached so many leaders on these types of conversations that the antics, tactics, and responses described are composites of real-life conversations and situations. For obvious reasons, the names and details have been altered. Regardless, you will quickly relate to the banter that will come in script-like form, providing all the back-and-forth dialogue that our two fictional characters might say to one another.

THE ANALYSIS

Each conversation will feature two fictional characters who display the extremes of a given DISC profile. For example, in one conversation, we might see a High-D speaking with a High-I. In another, a High-C might speak to a High-S, and so on. Each of the 7 Dreaded Conversations will include a different combination of profiles. Seeing each of the profiles interacting with each other will help you pick up more of the skills it takes to identify profiles quickly.

PERFORMANCE PRINCIPLE

Here, I will outline all the reasons that one or both of the characters in each conversation failed to conduct the conversation effectively. These are all the lessons on what they did wrong, so that we might learn how to do it better. Each chapter will feature a unique call-out lesson displayed in a gray box—these lessons are based on research, psychology principles, my own experiences and client testimonials—all lessons that make my work better and more customized than a simple internet search of DISC. Keep in mind that these lessons can (and often do) apply to every Dreaded Conversation. In this way, they are lessons that will build on each other and help supplement your growing expertise in communicating with each profile.

SAY THIS!

Now we get down to the nuts and bolts of how to conduct this Dreaded Conversation in a more effective way. As you will see, the strategy for each conversation's resolution has three parts. They are:

1. THE APPROACH

This is all about how to set the right expectations before you even engage with a particular profile. What tone does the conversation need to take? From which angle should you approach? What will this person think once they realize what this difficult conversation is about?

Certain performance profiles want it delivered simple and straight—no beating around the bush. Others need their ego stroked a bit. It's important to know which profile is which, because if you get it wrong, you could send your conversation partner off on a very unproductive path (or worse, you could cause that person to smell your BS from a mile away, and then they'll wind up thinking you're a pushover).

2. THE PITCH

Here we will cover exactly how to execute the targeted message we're seeking for every Dreaded Conversation. This section in each chapter will provide you with the very specific items that must be stated, along with some key ideas that will help solve the conversation's unique challenges.

3. THE WIN

Should you expect everyone to thank and praise you for telling them they need to shape up? No! While some might thank you for the talk, you certainly won't get that pleasantry or respect from everyone. In the chapters to come, this section will outline exactly what the Win looks like for each profile in each of the seven most Dreaded Conversations.

THE PROFILES

Of course, not every Dreaded Conversation fits into the same neat little box involving the same two profiles. So, in this section, I will provide tips for how to Approach, Pitch, and Win that specific Dreaded Conversation with all four performance profiles.

In addition to the standard structure above, some chapters will include call-out lessons that will further enhance your knowledge of how to conduct these conversations in a more productive manner.

Make sense? Great! Then let's begin.

PART 2

THE 7 DREADED CONVERSATIONS

DREADED CONVERSATION #1

SOMEBODY MESSED UP. HOW DO I TELL THEM?

We need to talk.

These four words can halt productivity, hinder performance, affect culture, and cost you a tremendous amount of time and money. Everyone knows that these words are code for "trouble is coming." But watch out! If you handle this conversation without regard for the other person's performance profile, then you risk a prolonged, costly mess.

Our first step toward getting further, faster, and being more effective as a leader is to figure out how to have this inevitable conversation in a way that both corrects the mistake (this is the easy part) and keeps the target profile *productive* (this is the hard part).

THE CONVERSATION

PARTICIPANTS

- » **AMY**, a manager with a budget-related problem
- » **KEVIN**, the firm's top salesperson

LOCATION

- » Amy's corner office
- » Floor-to-ceiling windows that allow everyone in the office to see into Amy's office

AMY (LEADER)

Kevin, get into my office now! We need to talk.

Kevin enters, keeping the door wide open.

KEVIN (SALESPERSON)

Is everything okay, Amy?

AMY (LEADER)

No. Everything is not okay! I've told you over and over that we're cutting costs and that you need to watch out for how much you're spending to entertain clients this quarter. But here I have last month's expense report. Apparently, you thought that taking two guys from Smith Brothers to dinner for $750 was a good idea.

Wrong decision! You're cut off! Give me your credit card. No more expense account for you.

Kevin doesn't reply. He just hands the credit card to Amy and then quietly walks out of her office.

THE ANALYSIS

Now that we've watched our two characters interact, let's take a step back and see what we can figure out about their performance profiles. Again, to make this more practical and user friendly, we don't need to run a full, precise mockup of each profile—rather, we're looking for big-picture signals.

Note: It is extremely important to improve your ability to read others. The more you learn about how to diagnose these profiles, the easier it will be for you to manage each of our seven most Dreaded Conversations.

AMY IS A HIGH-D (DRIVER)

Here's how we know:

1. When Kevin asked a question of concern, Amy gave a quick and confrontational retort. In other words, Amy had no problem upping the ante in confrontational conversation.
2. She made inexact generalizations about what she told Kevin regarding the new spending policy.
3. With statements like, "Wrong decision," she demonstrated a willingness to demean with sarcasm.
4. She delivered a swift judgment, followed by an immediate execution of the punishment.

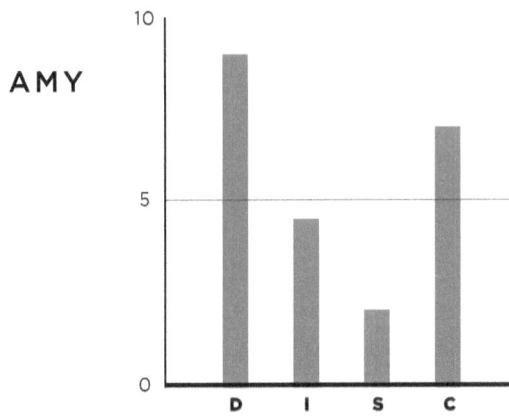

KEVIN IS A HIGH-S (STABILIZER)

1. He didn't respond negatively to Amy's aggressive demand to "get into his office." Rather, his immediate response was to express concern.
2. Kevin is obviously a socially engaging person. We learned he has a track record of entertaining clients. So then, why are we calling him a High-S profile rather than a High-I profile, which is usually the profile most likely to be described as the life of the party? There is a key distinction. We did not observe Kevin having any

highly animated gestures or an overly optimistic attitude, and we didn't hear an attempt to talk his way out of this situation or laugh it off. These are classic traits of a High-I, and they're missing from Kevin's personality. So, while Kevin is a "people person," he's more of a High-S than a High-I profile.

3. He spent $750 on a meal for three people, an exorbitant expense in almost any restaurant. In other words, Kevin was trying to impress his clients by taking them to a high-class establishment. Either that or the expenses of the evening spiraled out of control because Kevin had a hard time saying "no."

4. Because he's had to be told about his spending habits more than once, Kevin either demonstrates a blatant disregard for this rule or is compulsively unable to adhere to it. This means one of three things: he doesn't worry about the penalty for spending too much; he gets too caught up in the excitement of entertaining clients; or he is so conflict-averse that he inadvertently allows others to take advantage of him.

5. Kevin handed over his credit card and walked away quietly without pressing the matter or arguing his side.

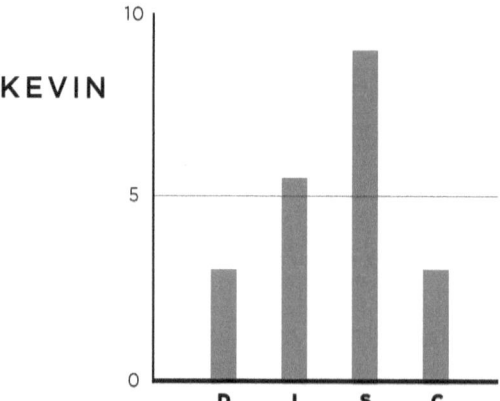

PERFORMANCE PRINCIPLE

Stop, Drop, and Roll

Amy certainly delivered a strong message to Kevin. There is no doubt that Kevin understands the point she was trying to make... Well, wait a second... What exactly does Kevin understand? Do you think he'll go back to his desk and say to himself, "Wow, Amy is right! I really messed up. Why did I do such a stupid thing? I better really bust my butt now and bring in extra revenue this month to make up for my mistake."

Because of Kevin's High-S profile, it is far more likely that Amy's actions will lead to a downturn in Kevin's performance for the next few days. But the worst part is that Amy missed a key leadership communication opportunity here, an opportunity to meet the three goals that every "you messed up" conversation should convey: Stop, Drop and Roll. We need to:

> **STOP** the situation that led to this conversation.
> **DROP** the bad habit, action, or attitude.
> **ROLL** forward with better performance, improved results, and a positive attitude.

While this Stop, Drop, and Roll performance principle is the same for every profile, the planning and preparation for each is unique. I can't stress this enough: if you don't sit and spend some time on how to engage each profile—and instead, you just wing it—then you're setting yourself up for disaster. The bulk of your success with mastering these Dreaded Conversations depends on how you approach the profiles.

SAY THIS!

Now that you know this performance principle, you can see why Amy failed in her first attempt. Let's take a look at a more effective strategy in leading Kevin.

How to approach a high-S (Stabilizer)

- » The Stabilizer doesn't like conflict. This means that Kevin is very sensitive and highly dedicated to others. Like other Stabilizers, he often talks in terms of "we" when discussing the company, the department, or the team.
- » The Stabilizer is process oriented. A common phrase you'll hear them use is, "That's the way we've always done it." For this reason, it is more likely that the mistake resulted from forgetting that a new process was put into place, even if you've repeatedly stated the change. The Stabilizer is usually under the impression that his actions were necessary to ensure thoroughness or relationship-building.
- » The Stabilizer will be upset about the mistake, upset that your feelings were hurt, and upset about the idea that he may have let the team or organization down.
- » As you prepare your approach, beware the Stabilizer's long memory. Whatever you say will be filed away in their brain. This means that, in a future confrontation, the Stabilizer won't get hysterical. Rather, he will get historical. He will start pulling up facts from 1987, or from a conversation you had five years ago, or from company policies that have been around since the founding, and so on.

How to pitch a high-S (Stabilizer)

- » When you call the Stabilizer into your office, it's best not to make it sound like the sky is falling. Just keep an even, friendly tone as you gently mention that you need to have a conversation.
- » **Important note**: Yelling is *not* the way to motivate the Stabilizer. If you yell, he will mentally shut down and become the most unproductive employee on staff for the next three days!
- » That said, we're not trying to sugarcoat anything here. We still need Kevin to know that the mistake was made, and it can't happen again. Firm, friendly, and clear—not harsh. That's the mantra here.

- » After a friendly greeting, transition your tone toward the concerns (but do it softly). "Well, I do have one concern," is the segue.
- » Whatever your words, they shouldn't be too abrupt or too harsh. You should frame things in a way that suggests you have a concern and you're looking for the Stabilizer's help in resolving it. Remember, the High-S *wants* to help people and will be *concerned* about your concern.
- » Here's a critical step: ask about the situation that has led to this problem, and then let the Stabilizer tell his story. Stabilizers like to explain, so let them explain (and don't be surprised if he tells a long story).
- » When he's finished explaining (or, at least, after a reasonable amount of his story has been shared), you should transition into a discussion of where the company, group, or team will be heading next. Stabilizers respond well to conversations about relationships, processes, and the overall structure of things. So this is where your side of the conversation should start: what's best for the group and why are we taking these steps forward.
- » Focus a lot of time on *why*. Explain why the policy or action is necessary to help us all win.
- » Now, it's important not to focus your *why* strictly on the corporate side of things. Focus it on how it will impact the people the Stabilizer works with. For example, you could say, "We don't want these expenses to continue or we might face layoffs. We have a good team here. I think we can agree that we don't want to see anybody have to leave."
- » The goals of this conversation should be to let the Stabilizer subtly know that if he doesn't drop the behavior, it will create a negative impact on others.
- » Tell the Stabilizer that you are here to help him in any way he needs to implement this action. He will want to feel supported, and like he's not on his own to deal with this challenge. That means you may want to offer a tag-team approach. Could you send an email (with him cc'd)? Could you personally attend the next meeting and kick it off in order to present a united front?

Whatever you can do to help and support the Stabilizer to fully implement the new process, you should do it.

» This may feel like too much handholding, but you won't need to do it forever. This is just a supportive measure to successfully launch the Stabilizer past the initial pain of putting this policy into action.

» Lastly, before you end the conversation, make sure the Stabilizer knows that everyone—not just you—appreciates his work, effort, and support.

With all of that in mind, let's return to Kevin and imagine yourself in Amy's shoes. Here is what a more effective version of this Dreaded Conversation should look like:

> **YOU** (LEADER)
> Kevin, may I speak with you about something I need your help on?
>
> **KEVIN** (EMPLOYEE)
> Sure, how can I help?
>
> **YOU** (LEADER)
> [In a calm, nonthreatening, relaxed tone] First, I'm curious to know about your son's baseball team. Are they tournament-bound?
>
> **KEVIN** (EMPLOYEE)
> Oh, we hope so. Mike is excited. He has a really nice coach, and he's played with these kids for a few years now, so they're really in sync.
>
> **YOU** (LEADER)
> That's great! What memories you're making.
>
> **KEVIN** (EMPLOYEE):
> So, what's going on?

YOU (LEADER)

Well, I was going through the expense reports and noticed that you took the guys from Smith Brothers out to dinner last week. How'd it go?

KEVIN (EMPLOYEE)

We had a lovely time. They're really nice guys, and they care a lot about the Main Street project. Actually, they were telling me that the project really got started when [at this point, Kevin will go on at length and recall, in sequential order, the conversation he had with the clients].

YOU (LEADER)

That's some great insight. I'm sure they appreciated you taking a sincere interest in their work. And I bet they also appreciated that fancy dinner, yeah?

KEVIN (EMPLOYEE)

Yeah.

YOU (LEADER)

If anyone can make a client feel valued, it's you. You have a real knack for it. It helps our company create great, lasting partnerships. And since our business goes through up and down cycles, those long-term relationships are important. It's been that way for years. But as you've heard me say lately, we're currently in one of those lukewarm zones—neither up nor down. So I was a little surprised when I saw that the bill for the dinner was $750. I'm not sure...

did you see the email I sent out a few weeks back about cutting down on our entertainment expenses?

KEVIN (EMPLOYEE)
I did.

YOU (LEADER)
Well, look: I know you just wanted to take care of a good client, but we're in that transition phase of the cycle, and we need to scale back on those entertainment dollars. If we can stick to our budget this quarter, we're going to be in a safer and more secure position to tackle the end-of-year crunch that always hits us. Do you know what I mean?

KEVIN (EMPLOYEE)
Oh, I know all about that. Fifteen years with this company.

YOU (LEADER)
So you know how people get this time of year. That's why we need to watch the dollars right now. We don't want there to be a strain on the system later on. That will only add to everyone's stress. Does that make sense?

KEVIN (EMPLOYEE)
Certainly does.

YOU (LEADER)
Good. But I also know you enjoy thinking of others and making nice gestures. So please

don't stop what you're doing. Let's just scale it back for the rest of the quarter to $500 a month—total. Okay?

KEVIN (EMPLOYEE)
Sounds good. And thank you, because I really do enjoy making people feel special.

YOU (LEADER)
And, how about this, the next time you're entertaining a customer and you think the spending might get out of control, blame me for the policy. It's okay to throw me under the bus in that situation. In fact, you can even spin it by saying, "Our company doesn't want to raise prices and hurt customers, so my boss has capped our credit cards."

KEVIN (EMPLOYEE)
Oh, I like the ring of that—we're looking out for them.

THE WIN WITH A HIGH-S (STABILIZER)

» The Stabilizer will depart with the understanding that he wants to change. He wants to be a team player, but he will be conflicted on how this will get done. Your offer of support during your pitch will be of great help to him as he comes to terms with this information about the mistake and how he is expected to fix it.
» Stabilizers are so relationship-driven that sometimes outside influences can cause them to make mistakes. You're going to have to help the High-S work through the conversation he will need to have with other people so that he can avoid making the mistake again.
» The more you can help the High-S think through things and feel like this is a team-oriented approach to finding the resolution,

the better off you will be. Continue to support him however you can, including offering frequent reminders about how valuable he is to both you and the company.

» Follow up from time to time over the next week or two to ask how he's doing, whether he's facing any challenges, and offering reminders that you are a supportive and sympathetic resource for him. Put another way, that first conversation with a Stabilizer shouldn't be the end of the conversation. There needs to be some follow up, sympathy, and encouragement.

THE PROFILES

Now that we've mastered the Approach, Pitch, and Win for a High-S like Kevin, let's see what they look like for the other three profiles.

HOW TO APPROACH A HIGH-D

» The Driver won't mind hearing about how she messed up. She puts on her big-girl pants every day, so you don't need to worry about hurting her feelings.

» The Driver thinks about it like this: "If I keep making this mistake, then it negatively impacts my productivity and return on investment." Since she is most concerned with achieving ultimate productivity, she will want to fix the problem as quickly as possible.

» At the same time, it's likely that the Driver will think your rule is stupid. Drivers don't think fondly of rules—especially ones they believe are so bureaucratic that they will slow down the rocket ride. So when you address the Feeling side of the conversation, be sure to highlight why the rule is neither slow nor stupid but maximizes profit and progress.

HOW TO PITCH A HIGH-D

- » The Driver is a hard worker with a great work ethic, but her primary concern is with the end product and *not* with the method of achieving it. Take special care to make her understand where she went wrong and why this is costing her (and likely the business) time and money.
- » **Be careful!** If you get too detailed about the process, you're going to lose the Driver's attention. Keep your message simple and straightforward.
- » With a High-D, there's a fine line between blunt/aggressive and rude/disrespectful, and it's very easy to cross. "Get in my office now, you piece of #%^&" crosses it. "We need to talk now" walks it pretty much perfectly.
- » Be sure to explain *why*. Now, it should not be a thirty-minute rant on *why*. Do this and *you'll lose their focus*. Rather, it should be a solid explanation of *why*, one that gives the High-D a sense of mission to take ownership of the mistake and make sure it doesn't happen again. Whether in the office or in front of your children, "Because I said so" is never anywhere near as effective as explaining *why* a certain behavior isn't okay and *why* it needs to be corrected.
- » Give her a goal to work toward. The Driver is very goal- and outcome-oriented.
- » You may want to point out that you feel betrayed by this behavior. Drivers have a high sense of honor. If you mention your offense, the High-D will pay closer attention to the issue at hand.

THE WIN WITH A HIGH-D

- » Don't expect the Driver to thank you. In fact, since she's not afraid to tell it like it is or use raw language, don't be completely surprised if she says *"F#%k you."* The Driver is rarely afraid to tell you how she feels about your "stupid little rule."
- » Expect her to appear irritated. Don't be surprised if the volume of her voice goes up. She might push back and argue with you.

- » Don't expect the Driver to go away happy and with a smile. At best, she will just *go*. Anticipate her to leave with a huff and a puff.
- » Now, I need you to be honest with yourself. If you're a less assertive boss—if you've been known to let things slide when someone acts out of turn—then I wouldn't be surprised if the High-D employee disregards the talk you just had. Drivers don't like anything that *feels* slow or stupid. It drives them crazy. They sometimes think that certain rules don't apply to them (namely, the rules they deem "slow and stupid" enough to impede their "get it done" mantra). So if you're not the most forceful boss, you may want to monitor the Driver's actions for a while to make sure she complies with your rule.
- » If you're a stronger boss, then I would suspect that while the Driver may not like your rule, she will follow it immediately.

(INFLUENCER)

HOW TO APPROACH A HIGH-I

- » The Influencer always wants to be the star or the hero, so he won't like hearing about messing up. He always wants to do well, but also has a tendency to focus more on his own success than that of the organization.
- » The Influencer also tends to be a people-pleaser. He wants everyone to like and recognize him.
- » Important Note: You can use the Influencer's desire for celebrity to make this situation a win for everyone.
- » Be careful! The Influencer also tends to focus too much on the good. They are eternal optimists who are highly unlikely to even be aware of the mistake before you raise the issue. If you go in with a scowl, it will put him on the defensive and set off alarm bells before you even speak.
- » Having a Dreaded Conversation with anyone is difficult, but for the High-I, having it in a public setting can be downright

painful. Public embarrassment has a unique way of shutting the Influencer down. In this situation, it would be better to close the blinds and shut the door so no one can see, and best to conduct the meeting in a place that is far from the prying eyes of the Influencer's coworkers and customers.

HOW TO PITCH A HIGH-I

- » Influencers are chock full of stories, anecdotes, and jokes. When you point out the mistake, it's often best to use a story or two to explain the situation and what should happen in the future.
- » Also, be sure to discuss some other areas where the Influencer did a good job. Stroke his ego, in other words.
- » The best pitch for an Influencer starts out with a congenial opening like, "Hey, Carl, could you come to my office? I'd like to talk to you for a few minutes." Deliver it with a smile, where possible. Where not possible, at least put on the kind of face and tone that doesn't scream danger. We don't want the Influencer or any of his coworkers to think he's in trouble.
- » Once the conversation starts, ask about specifics first. "So, how did the dinner with the Smith Brothers reps go?"
- » It's important to let the Influencer explain himself first. They love telling stories, after all. Make sure you *enjoy* the story, even if you're seething inside about the mistake. Just hold tight. Let the Influencer be himself. We need him to engage before he will understand the mistake.
- » With story-time over, now we can shift the tone, discuss the mistake, and let him know *why* we need to avoid a situation like this again. "It sounds like you had a great time, but I saw the bill for the dinner was $750" is the tone to strike. The Influencer might try to defuse the situation or explain why the decision was necessary. Let it happen. Then get into the *why* it is important to stop this behavior.
- » Ideally, while you're describing the necessary change, it helps to have a story about how someone else made this same adjustment and was still effective. On the other side, it also helps to have a

story of someone who met with failure because they *didn't* make the change you're requesting. Examples and stories, both positive and negative, will resonate strongly with the Influencer.

» The Influencer wants to be the hero, so use his inner desire to your advantage. Position him and this conversation in a number of ways: you are *the* person everyone is looking at to set their pace with this policy; you are the only guy who is capable of doing this and saving the company's quarterly earnings report; our customers want to work with you—it's your charm and personality they crave, not some $100 steak; or (on the slightly more negative side), "I know you like going out with the high-rollers and it's part of your tremendous success, so I don't want to have to take the credit card away and stop all entertainment. But I will if you can't get this under control."

THE WIN WITH A HIGH-I

» He is going to want to leave on a positive, friendly note. The Influencer will probably make a flippant comment, tell some joke as he walks out of your office, or change the subject to something much more neutral or favorable.
» You might question if he understands the gravity of your talk, but his apparent deflection is likely just a defense mechanism.
» Also, don't be surprised if the Influencer wears his emotions on his sleeves during this talk.
» Influencers don't want anyone to know they messed up. They do all they can to avoid public ridicule. Remember, they want to be seen and recognized as important and fun.
» The High-I will face three big challenges after leaving your office:
  › First, he is going to need a way to save face in front of others who are wondering why the boss called him into the office. You can help him here by ending your talk with, "Now, you keep up the great job impressing those clients with your charm and expertise." In essence, you're priming the Influencer's thoughts so that, when he walks out, he can say the boss wanted to tell him what a great job he's been doing.

You could even walk him out of your office saying these things for others to hear.
> Second, the Influencer will want to save face in front of his clients. You could let him figure this one out on his own. Don't be shocked if you later hear through the grapevine that the Influencer told someone he can't spend money because the boss is being tough. Keep in mind that what may sound like the Influencer throwing you under the bus is far more likely to have been a comment made jokingly with a smile.
> Third, the High-I will struggle with remembering the policy or avoiding getting caught up in a spending spree. Influencers want to impress and have fun. They also get distracted easily. So if you know that your High-I is going to be talking to some clients he normally takes out for a bite to eat, you may want to give him a subtle reminder of your talk. Just be sure you do this in private, so he doesn't feel embarrassed.

C (CONSCIENTIOUS)

HOW TO APPROACH A HIGH-C

» The Conscientious profile doesn't make mistakes (at least that's what he would like you to think). Now, of course, everyone makes mistakes, it's just that a High-C doesn't like to admit to them. In fact, every mistake he makes cuts to his heart.
» The High-C is extremely logical (I'm talking, like, Spock from *Star Trek*) and detail-oriented (they make great lawyers and engineers), so you better make sure your case is well prepared. Getting him to admit that he was wrong takes a *lot* of proof.
» The Conscientious profile has a high regard for compliance and rules. If you failed to be specific in your new policy, he will certainly bring that fact up.

- » The High-C loves to debate—the more theoretical, the better. This makes him more prone to latch onto logic and less prone to be swayed by emotions. This doesn't mean that he is emotionless; rather he tends to focus on evidence over feelings. This can sometimes manifest itself in the form of "intellectual sarcasm," or an effort to frame your argument as illogical or ill conceived.
- » On the other hand, once you provide proof and make your case, the High-C will follow your request to a T (even if they may not be happy with the rule).
- » **Important Note**: Think of engaging a High-C in a "mistake" conversation as if you're preparing to argue before the Supreme Court.

HOW TO PITCH A HIGH-C

- » As soon as you utter the words, "You're wrong," prepare for battle! So don't say, "You're wrong," even though he *is* wrong. We're trying to create a conducive environment where the High-C will truly hear you, and we can't get there by immediately giving him reason to put up his defenses.
- » Beware of making an argument that's rooted in "Because I said so." If you do this, the High-C might stop making the mistake in the future, but he might also start a quiet mutiny within the office based on your "incompetence and illogical ways."
- » Being matter of fact and to the point is fine for the C. But don't forget the detail. The High-C is all about detail. Because he is so focused on detail, it's best to *start* this conversation with facts. In our example, if Kevin (the employee) were a High-C, the best pitch would have started with, "I see that you spent $750 last evening with Smith Brothers."
- » Next, it is best to keep the ball in the Conscientious profile's court by asking him if he was aware of the rule in question. If he wasn't aware, then your conversation is nearly over. Just share the rule and the High-C will be likely to follow it in future.
- » If he was aware of the rule, however, then we may have a problem, because it was likely violated as a result of him thinking that it was flawed somehow.

- » In addressing why the policy is the policy, you want to focus on the logical aspects. There is an approximately equal chance that the High-C will agree with your logic as there is that he will believe it is flawed. If it's the latter, expect some pushback on what he believes is the more logical way.
- » In the end, if the Conscientious profile is still resistant to accepting the logic and reasoning behind your policy and correction, then offer him a metaphorical carrot. Let him know that when he has the bandwidth, he is welcome to research, find, and present a new way to do things so that the rule could be changed to his liking. But until then, the existing rule is in place.

THE WIN WITH A HIGH-C

- » The win here can go either way. If he is on board with your logic, he will walk out and be the absolute ambassador for this policy. If he doesn't agree with the logic, he will walk out with an icy and unsettled, "Well, if that's what you want." But he will also be motivated to move forward on your offer to research and prove there's a better way than your current position.
- » In the meantime, he will likely adhere to your rule. In fact, he will probably hold to the very letter of the law, if nothing more than to prove the perceived absurdity of your rule.
- » If he is going to keep your rule but remain intellectually opposed on this issue, then how do you keep him productive? Follow up with him! Persistently ask if he's researched alternative solutions that he is ready to present. If he has, they will probably be really good alternatives to consider. And if he hasn't looked into this, perhaps he has decided to let it go, accept the inevitability of the change, and move forward.

DREADED CONVERSATION #2

SOMEONE ASKED ME FOR A RAISE. HOW DO I TURN THEM DOWN?

When you're in the decision-maker's chair, you face some tough questions. Sometimes those questions require intense research and hard choices. Other times, they are just plain awkward. This is one of those times. When someone asks for a raise and they don't deserve it, how do we say no without breaking their spirit to keep working?

One of my clients who runs an oil and gas company was recently approached by someone asking for a raise. After a review with HR, this leader discovered that it had been ten years since the last raise for this particular role. Cases like these are no-brainers. But, of course, these matters are rarely so clear cut.

There are plenty of occasions when eager, ambitious, forthright people have approached their bosses with requests to be paid more. In these situations, it's so easy to fall into the knee-jerk reaction and either give this person a flat no or stall for time by telling them that you will review it soon and get back to them at a later, unspecified date. These reactions can eliminate the problem in the immediate, but they can also create problems under the surface—namely productivity issues as time passes because the employee feels put off and unappreciated.

Yes, some people will stick with a job (at least for a while) because of a great boss, nice incentives, opportunities for career advancement, and so on, but at the end of the day, money is a major facet of work. It says something about a person's value, position, the lifestyle they live, and what they can provide for their family. So if we have to say no to a raise, the most important thing we can do is deliver the news in a way that moves the person forward, keeps them productive, and provides a positive outlook. So let's dive into the best way to break the news to each profile.

THE CONVERSATION

Participants

- » **DAVE**, a salesperson for a global telecommunications company
- » **MARIA**, the VP of sales

Location

- » Dave approaches Maria in her office, completely unannounced.

DAVE (SALESPERSON)
Hey Maria. I love that outfit! Listen, I'll get straight to it. I've been working here now for three years, and every quarter, I'm near the top of the sales performance charts. And now I've got a baby on the way. My wife and I are really excited. We've been out every weekend shopping at baby stores and picking out all those fun toys and items. Our little girl is going to be thrilled with her princess room! Well, anyway, my wife and I were talking at Starbucks the other day and I realized that it's been a while since I've had a raise.

MARIA (LEADER)
[caught off guard] First off, congratulations on the baby. Secondly, I hadn't given this

any thought before this moment. I'll need to talk to HR and figure it out.

DAVE (SALESPERSON)
I understand. That's all I ask, but please keep in mind that I've been selling in the toughest sector of our business and I've established phenomenal relationships with three new top-tier customers this year and I really think these guys are going to put in a huge order soon. Plus, I gave that great talk at the trade show last month. Everyone loved it and said it was the best presentation on the Core-It product they've heard yet! Also—

MARIA (LEADER)
[interrupting] You said you've been here three years?

DAVE (SALESPERSON)
Yes. I started in January of—

MARIA (LEADER)
[interrupting again] I know you're out there selling and hitting the pavement, but the truth is that the budget is tight. I think there's a process for all this anyway. If you started in January, then that's when your next performance review will happen.

DAVE (SALESPERSON)
But January is when Janine is due. I really need a raise now. Or as close to now as you can manage. I have some big plans for baby's room and—

MARIA (LEADER)
[flatly] Your last review showed improvement. But is it to the level we needed?

DAVE (SALESPERSON)
If you look at how I've done this year, I think you'll see that—

MARIA (LEADER)
[interrupting] You just have to give me more time, Dave. Let me dig into the numbers and get back to you. I'm sympathetic. Really. But please don't get your hopes up. Money is tight.

With that, Maria hastily departs for her next meeting, leaving Dave in the dust. She doesn't notice this at the time, but Dave is more than a little miffed by the response. The answer he received was almost worse than a straightforward "no," because now he hasn't gotten a real answer, and he hasn't received any sense of direction or anticipation of when that answer will come. For however long it takes for Maria to make up her mind (if she even plans to follow up on the question), Dave is going to feel jaded, undervalued, and underappreciated. This will impact his performance, and it might even spill over and impact the morale of the rest of Dave's team.

THE ANALYSIS

DAVE IS A HIGH-I (INFLUENCER)

Here's how we know:

1. He was more than excited to share the news of his weekend shopping activities with his wife, and also specifically mentioned a conversation he had in a Starbucks.

2. The word "I" frequently came up in his side of the conversation, and the results he cited focused more on image and relationships than concrete outcomes.
3. He was proud to point out his accomplishments and success (even if they didn't live up to Maria's expectations).

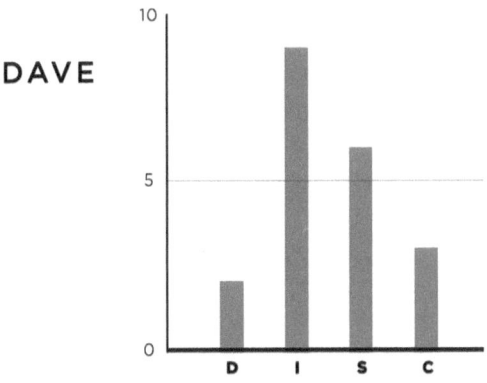

MARIA IS A HIGH-D (DRIVER)

1. She was curt and to the point.
2. Interrupting Dave happened frequently and without hesitation.
3. She seemed most concerned with budget and results.
4. She had not done any research on the subject and didn't offer a sense that she had any real intention of following up.

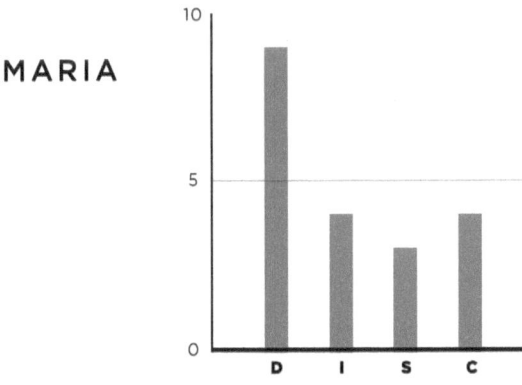

PERFORMANCE PRINCIPLE

Three E's of Rejecting a Raise

When you're approached for a raise, the only question is this: Are you getting the performance that warrants the raise? This is a far more objective, factual way to approach the subject than the subjective, wish-washy reaction some leaders give.

To get to that point where you come across as objective and factual, you must address three key elements, or the Three E's of Rejecting a Raise. You have to Empathize, Explain, and show the Endzone.

1. EMPATHIZE

Do more than just listen to the request and then shoot it down. Dig a little deeper into the why this person needs a raise. Their answers might surprise you. As a benefit, doing this demonstrates your willingness to thoughtfully consider the request while also buying you some time to think.

Remember that at some point in your life, assuming you are a leader or a senior executive, you have been in this person's situation. Recalling this will help you more authentically relate the fact that you get it. Briefly (and I do mean briefly) say something to the effect of, "I know what you mean. I was in that same situation when I was in my late twenties."

Important caveat: *don't* say, "Here's how I got through it." Why? Because they're *not* you. They may not want to take the same action as you did. The goal is to show that you can relate to their desire for a raise and connect to their emotions. This is not the time or place to give advice.

2. EXPLAIN

Here is where you explain *why* they can't get a raise right now.

If you *don't* know the answer at the moment, that's fine. Tell them that. "Let me go and look into the numbers and see what I can do. Let's circle back on this within the week." This way, you don't dismiss the request so quickly that it seems like you don't care about the person. You're demonstrating that you fully intend to offer them a real chance and an objective review.

If you *do* know the answer, then perhaps you can answer in the moment. Just make sure they know that you have direct, recent insight into their performance numbers and your objective, honest opinion is that the current numbers don't reflect a raise.

Be sure to match your explanation to the profile. If you tell a Driver that he isn't getting a raise because it won't look good to others who think they should also get a raise, that message won't resonate with the High-D, who is all about results, not about what other people think. Conversely, talking exclusively about results with a Stabilizer isn't going to be as effective as explaining how the whole team is struggling and we're trying to help everyone out but there's just not a ton of budget to go around. More on these points as we examine each profile below.

3. ENDZONE

This is probably the most critical part of the talk because it's where we can make our "no" seem more like a "yes." Okay, so you just broke it to this person that they aren't meeting the performance standards you need. Now you get to show them how they can achieve that performance and get what they want. You're showing them the goal line they must cross to get the raise.

You should always be willing to pay for performance, so this Endzone should be based on an objective performance metric. Each profile tends to struggle with its own things, so the Profile sections to come will highlight what to look for.

First, though, one final point: when this conversation is over, no one is going to be thrilled. Don't expect this news to be received with open arms, no matter what the profile. No one likes to hear that they haven't earned a raise. But if you do this right, then you'll show them that you support their needs, intend to help them when they've earned it, and just as importantly, you have provided a pathway to the "yes" that they so desire.

SAY THIS!

Since Dave's profile is an Influencer, let's first examine the Approach, Pitch, and Win associated with a more effective conversation with a High-I.

How to approach a High-I (Influencer)

- » Performance occurs on a spectrum. One side measures a person's productivity while the other side measures their contribution to culture and positivity.
- » With this in mind, it is likely that a High-I like Dave has great appeal on the positive-culture side but is not quite as productive as he thinks he is.
- » The High-I is usually well liked and well-polished, but usually overestimates his results/outcomes. One might say he has a tendency to be all smoke and mirrors. Of course, you don't want to actually say this to him, but it's probably the issue that will prevent him from getting a raise today.
- » The conversation will need to let him know that he has great appeal on one side of the performance equation, but unfortunately, we're not yet getting as much as we want on the productivity side.

How to pitch a High-I (Influencer)

- » **The Endzone**: Be prepared with a specific, objective measurement that he needs to achieve. Maybe it's a number of widgets sold. Maybe it's the number of calls made/answered/resolved. Many Influencers are capable of achieving results, but generally lack speed and focus toward them.
- » Have an example of somebody who is already achieving the results/performance you expect. Important caveat: make it clear to the Influencer that you're not trying to *make* him into that specific example person. You're just trying nudge him closer to that level of performance.

Here's what that looks like in action:

DAVE (EMPLOYEE)

Hi, Maria. Listen, I'll get straight to it. I've been working here now for three years, and every quarter, I'm near the top of the sales performance charts. I've got a baby on the way. I need a raise.

YOU (LEADER)

That's fantastic news! You're going to be a great father. I bet Janine is really excited.

DAVE (EMPLOYEE)

Absolutely. Did I tell you the story about how she broke the news?

Dave will proceed to tell the story. Whether you've heard it already or not, just let him. Inject positive comments and jokes wherever possible. Build rapport and keep the conversation light.

YOU (LEADER)

[confidently] I can certainly sympathize with wanting a raise when you have a baby on the way. I've been in your shoes. But here's the thing: while it's true that you're getting the numbers, it's also true that we only give raises at performance review time, and yours won't be up until January.

DAVE (EMPLOYEE)

But January is when Janine is due with our little girl. I need a raise now. Plus, it's me we're talking about here—your superstar!

YOU (LEADER)

I respect that. But how is it going to look in front of the others if I give you a raise outside the usual process? It'll look like you're getting special favors. Not only will that negatively impact morale, but it could cause resentment toward you.

DAVE (EMPLOYEE)

I guess I hadn't thought of that.

YOU (LEADER)

Look, I know you're making sales. You reel in the big fish. That'll reflect well on your next review. But what I need from you is more consistency. If you can show a sense of urgency between now and January—if you can start landing more consistent sales for the next six months—then next review will reflect well, and you'll be in line for what you want.

DAVE (EMPLOYEE)

So you want me to stop chasing the big fish?

YOU (LEADER)

[smiling] Not at all. We're just looking for you to balance out those big fish with some smaller fish on a more regular basis. Think about Nora. She's up there in the numbers with you, but her client orders are more consistent. She has a few big fish, but lots of smaller ones too. That provides stability, which we appreciate. If you can balance

your client load like Nora while also keeping those big fish, then your salary next year will reflect that performance.

DAVE (EMPLOYEE)

So...you're telling me I have to wait?

YOU (LEADER)

[patiently] I am. But I'm also telling you that you're valued here, and that if you head in this direction, then we'll absolutely pay you for that performance.

THE WIN WITH A HIGH-I (INFLUENCER)

- » Either during the initial conversation or at some point over the next few weeks, the High-I will probably say that he has problems with achieving the Endzone you've established. This is because he likely believes that a huge part of his success comes from doing exactly what he has always done. In his view, changing in an effort to get to that equilibrium between productivity and positive culture will hinder his strengths and harm overall performance.
- » The answer to this is simple: "That's okay. We're looking for equilibrium. So some of what you do extremely well will have to diminish slightly. We're not looking for all or nothing here. As a high-performance organization, we're looking for balance."
- » The High-I is going to want to make you happy. This makes him the second most likely employee to accept the news in stride. But here, it's probably still only a 50/50 shot.
- » Eventually, though, his goal will be primarily to make you proud. If your message about the Endzone has resonated, then expect him to find the necessary motivation.

THE PROFILES

 **(DRIVER)**

How to Approach a High-D

» A High-D tends to get results at the expense of others. She performs well but also leaves a pile of bodies in her wake. A Driver's bluntness, aggressiveness, and uncouthness can cause other problems for the company. So, focus your approach on this collateral damage.
» Incentivize the desire for results but remind her that there is a delicate balance between high productivity and a positive culture. The message should be how, in a high-performance organization, there has to be a balance between the two. The Driver has probably erred way too far on the productivity side at the expense of the quality and cultural sides.
» Money is a major motivator for the High-D, and since you're going to tell her she can't get more money, it probably won't go over well at all. For this profile, the Endzone piece is the most important. So know the pathway before you make the final rejection.

How to Pitch a High-D

» **The Endzone**: Explain the specific, objective measurements (not subjective, emotional feelings) that she needs to achieve. Present a timeframe for when this will be remeasured and reevaluated.
» Don't try to sugarcoat it or buddy-buddy her before you deliver the boom. You don't have to be ice cold, but no-nonsense is necessary. Get straight to the point.
» Do it privately. No one else needs to know what someone is or isn't getting paid.

- » Bring the Driver back into equilibrium. ("I want a high-performance organization, which means I want a great balance between productivity and positive culture. So we need to talk about specific instances/examples where people have come up and complained about your attitude, approach, personality, and ways of achieving your goals.")
- » The Driver is all about time and results, so be very specific about what she needs to achieve and by when she needs to achieve it. Make sure to coach her on when she will have an opportunity to demonstrate this improved behavior. Don't be ambiguous about starting and ending points. ("You need to make ten widgets by next week and your next opportunity to do this is tomorrow morning when you walk through these doors." Or, "You need to go play with the accounting team effectively so I don't have more than two complaints in a month. I'll evaluate this at the end of the quarter.")
- » Provide an example of what the desired behavior looks like. You're not asking her to be exactly like this person. You're saying, "Hey, you're at the opposite end of the spectrum from where this person is, and I need you to get a little closer to balance."

The Win for a High-D

- » The High-D will look and act disgusted by the news. She might blow up at you a bit, might think you're a jerk, and might stew for a while after.
- » She's most likely not going to leave in a happy or even a neutral demeanor. She'll be more like, "Ugh! You've got to be kidding me." She might even use a few expletives. If you've assured her that there is a path to being paid more that comes through better performance, then you've won.

S (STABILIZER)

How to Approach a High-S

- » Out of all the profiles, the S will probably be the most balanced on the spectrum between productivity and positive culture. But she certainly won't be *perfectly* balanced. Most likely, she will be something like an 8 on the culture side and a 4 on productivity.
- » The Approach for the Stabilizer will be to make it clear that while her cultural contributions are invaluable, her productivity needs to improve. We're not looking for an 8/4 positive culture/productivity split, but at least a 6/6 balance.
- » On the productivity side, she will need to work faster, be more aggressive, make quicker decisions, and be more forward thinking. On the culture side, she will need to speak less, stop taking on too much (in other words, learn to say "no"), and better prioritize her time.

How to Pitch a High-S

- » **The Endzone**: Prepare to have a timeframe, objective standard, and example of how she can achieve balance, along with an example person who is already doing this. Tell her the next opportunity when she can demonstrate this new behavior.
- » The High-S enjoys being asked about how she's doing and feeling. So before you give your ultimate answer on the raise, request a couple minutes to discuss something that is a sensitive topic that you wanted to get back to her about after your fact-finding mission.
- » Keep a nonthreatening tone. You're bringing a process to fruition here. You promised, and now you're following back up. Stabilizers love this. They also love the personal touch. Make sure you say these things specifically. They resonate.

- » When it comes time to break the news, take it slow and be calm. Keep your tone soft.
- » In everything you say, talk about the team first. ("I'm just so proud of everything we've accomplished as a team.")
- » But then, once you've established how much you value her cultural contribution, it's time to lay out the performance metrics she has to meet if she wants the raise in the future.
- » Don't pressure the High-S for this performance. (Stabilizers don't like pressure.)

The Win with a High-S

- » While the High-S usually prefers to keep her emotions to herself, this is also the profile most likely to leave the conversation with a tear in her eye. Either way, you won't get much feedback. Stabilizers tend to be emotional, but they don't always wear those emotions on their sleeves.
- » In the days following the conversation, ask if she needs help. (This is actually good practice for all four profiles, but it's especially important for the Stabilizer.) Does she need coaching/training/resources? An ear to listen? Guidance? ("As a leader, what can I do to move you forward so that we can pay you for performance?") Sometimes people know what to do but simply do not know how to do it.

C (CONSCIENTIOUS)

How to Approach a High-C

- » The C is matter-of-fact, so don't warm up or sugarcoat it.
- » The High-C is going to lean more toward the productivity end of our spectrum, while his positive-culture side is going to be very lackluster. So, have some evidence about how he can improve his positive-culture performance.

» Your evidence may have to be anecdotal, which could raise a problem for the High-C. As such, you may need to be prepared with more than one story. The goal is to establish patterns related to the issues this Conscientious profile needs to fix.

How to Pitch a High-C

» **The Endzone**: This one is tougher, since it's a little more difficult to objectively measure cultural performance and positivity. In this case, your Endzone will need to include a timeframe in which the High-C can demonstrate that the problem patterns have been eliminated.
» He is going to want to get right to it. Where you can, provide data, evidence, and if you don't have that, then anecdotes. Just be sure to establish the pattern he has to overcome if he wants to get paid.
» For a High-C, this isn't a conversation. At best, he will treat it as an analysis; at worst, he will treat it as a head-on debate. Come equipped with plenty of evidence about the improvements that need to be made. And be prepared for a little pushback. The more you can anticipate his counterevidence, the better off you'll be.

The Win with a High-C

» This will go one of two ways.
  › He'll be very upset and think that your evidence is wrong. (In essence, the problem is not with him; the problem is with your stories, data, and/or expectations.)
  › Or he'll say (in highly analytical fashion), "Okay. Fine. I'll do what needs to be done."
» As long as you proved your point, showed him the Endzone, and offered to help, you've gotten the job done.

As a final note on the subject of turning down a request for a raise, remember that not everyone will accept your evidence and reasoning, or even agree with you. Think about it this way: no matter who the

President of the United States happens to be, just about half the country will think he's wrong and the other half will think he's doing just great. You can't please everyone all the time.

So, it's pretty unlikely that the recipient of this conversation will give you a hug and thank you for your analysis. They're just as likely to react in the opposite way. Just make sure you Empathize, Explain, and show them the Endzone. This formula will get you and them much further and faster while making both of you more effective.

DREADED CONVERSATION #3

SOMEONE HAS LOST THEIR MOJO. HOW DO I MOTIVATE THEM?

So you have to motivate someone who just isn't performing up to the standards you've come to expect. To achieve a Win for this conversation, you first need to put yourself in the mindset of the underperformer and then identify their primary motivators. Once you know what their psyche craves, it's all about how you frame the upcoming conversation to reignite and re-energize that all-important spark that drives their performance.

You can find plenty of "motivation assessments" on the Internet. They'll highlight drivers such as knowledge, socialization, utility, beauty, and a few others. But for our purposes, you should know that there is a strong correlation between each of the performance profiles and specific motivating forces. Granted, the following list isn't the end-all of factors that can motivate each person you work with, but if you identify your target's performance profile, then focusing on the following motivators will put you way ahead of the game.

Here are the primary motivators for each dominant profile:

» **High-D (Driver)**: Return on Investment (ROI), Money, and Movement
» **High-I (Influencer)**: Status, Recognition, and Being the Hero
» **High-S (Stabilizer)**: Consensus, Cooperation, and Duplication
» **High-C (Conscientious)**: Quality, Logic, and Being Right

Let's keep these motivators in mind as we examine how not to, and then how to, conduct this Dreaded Conversation.

THE CONVERSATION

PARTICIPANTS

- » **BILL**, the leader of a team of software developers with a rapidly approaching deadline
- » **JANET**, a coder who Bill doesn't think is working quickly enough

LOCATION

- » Janet's cubicle, with Bill standing over his employee's desk

> **BILL** (LEADER)
> Hey, J-lo. Let's talk about something.
>
> **JANET** (EMPLOYEE)
> Okay. My name is Janet, though.
>
> **BILL** (LEADER)
> [smiling] Sorry about that. Just trying to keep things loose. I have nicknames for everyone. Listen, I don't like having to say this, but I need you to complete your piece today, or we're gonna be up a creek, you know what I'm saying?
>
> It's like that time when Antonio was out on paternity leave, and we didn't have anybody in-house we could turn to for answers—
>
> **JANET** (EMPLOYEE)
> [furrowing her brow] I remember. But what does that have to do with me?

BILL (LEADER)

It's just that it's such a similar situation. There's no one else here who knows the Apple iOS quite like you, and you're the only one who can code in Swift. If I don't have your adjustments to the language on the social media share feature, our app's going to be crap.

JANET (EMPLOYEE)

Have you considered pushing the deadline? I mean, we're already breaking the rule on consecutive hours of coding here. I don't know who thought this deadline was possible in the first place. Obviously, they weren't thinking of the full project scope.

BILL (LEADER)

[touching Janet's shoulder] Yeah, yeah. But, Jan, this is my biggest client. And you know what happens if I don't keep them happy.

JANET (EMPLOYEE)

[pulling away from Bill's touch] Yes, but—

BILL (LEADER)

[interrupting] What happens is that Mark will look for someone to blame. The ax has to fall on someone, Jan, and it's not going to fall on me. I've worked too hard on this project. You don't want it to be you, do you?

JANET (EMPLOYEE)

No, of course not.

> **BILL** (LEADER)
> [in his best Clint Eastwood voice] Great. Then we understand each other. Let's get it going!

With that, Bill departs, confident that his careful application of the traditional motivational whipping stick of "you might just get fired," will compel Janet to improve her performance. Of course, given Janet's profile, Bill is completely fooling himself in this situation.

THE ANALYSIS

BILL IS A HIGH-I (INFLUENCER)

Here's how we know:

» From his insistence on using nicknames, dropping jokes to keep things light, employing a character voice, smiling and touching Janet's shoulder, we know he has a bit of swagger. He's a real character!
» He's long-winded and does his level best to frame his points with storytelling—hence his quick callback story to Antonio's paternity leave.
» He doesn't mind using a little flattery to get what he wants.
» He's clearly more optimistic about the team's ability to meet tough deadlines than is Janet.
» He seems far more concerned about how this situation is going to affect *him* specifically. Notice he said, "my client" instead of "our client," as well as pointing out that it's *he* who keeps the client happy, and how hard *he* has worked on this project, not the team.

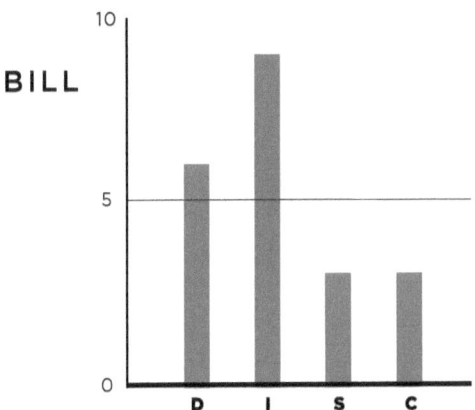

Janet is a High-C (Conscientious)

» She rigidly corrects and then requests that Bill call her by her given name.
» Her body language suggests an analytical nature. She doesn't like Bill's hand touching her shoulder.
» She seems to want to stick to the facts and is clearly looking for evidence that what is being asked of her can actually be achieved.
» She asks questions, references the rules about how things are supposed to be done, and doubts that the team ever had the ability to meet the deadline—even questioning the intellectual capacity of those who created the deadline.

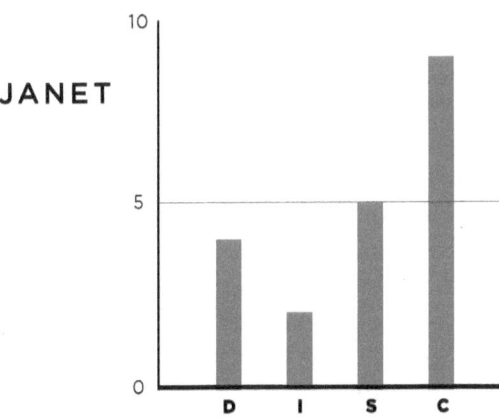

PERFORMANCE PRINCIPLE

Push/Pull

Bill made plenty of mistakes during his conversation with Janet, but the primary reason his Pitch won't produce the Win he is hoping for is this: he failed to recognize that there are two critical factors in motivating a person: push and pull.

Think about a car. The default drivetrain for most cars is either rear-wheel drive or front-wheel drive. Both have their upsides and downsides. If you're looking for speed, rear-wheel drive is where it's at, because the car is being pushed forward. But all that pushing power spells trouble if the weather conditions turn less than favorable. My brother Jonathan experienced this firsthand as he drove his bright yellow Mustang home one night in the rain. His muscle car quickly became a wimp in the downpour, and he slid all over the road. In this situation, Jonathan didn't need the classic pushing power of a sports car; he needed the pulling power of a front-wheel drive.

If you're in a front-wheel drive vehicle, you face the opposite problem. While you have plenty of control and stability during more challenging conditions, these cars just don't have the same power and "go" of the rear-wheel drive muscle cars.

This is exactly why four-wheel-drive cars, trucks, and SUVs are so popular. Whatever the situation may be, you get the best balance of power and stability when both *push* and *pull* are present.

The same concept applies to motivating someone. You can't just *push* with the punitive, like Bill did with Janet. Pushing others can indeed "light a fire" under their feet and get them going, but it's not enough on its own. When the conditions become difficult, no matter how much push is applied, the person will abandon the mission because they are not also being pulled by an internal desire that makes them *want* to achieve the goal. While there's plenty of research on this, I'll point to more practical case studies: ask any parent who has barked at their child to "study harder and get better grades" how that has worked out for them. You can yell all you want, but it won't serve as sufficient motivation on its own.

Likewise, you can't just pull someone forward by offering a reward. Pulling alone doesn't have enough power to get someone going. For example, many people struggle for years with a desire to have a better-looking physique. No matter what they try, they just can't seem to sustain an effort to get into shape. Similarly, why haven't you written that bestselling book that's been bounding inside your brain for all these years?

In these cases, you have a desire and want to produce something, yet you don't. Why? Because there's no one pushing you to get it done now! This is why the best strategy, no matter which profile you're speaking to, is to incorporate both the push and the pull into your Approach and Pitch to motivate someone.

SAY THIS!

Since Janet's profile is Conscientious, let's first examine the Approach, Pitch, and Win associated with a more effective conversation with a High-C.

How to Approach a High-C (Conscientious)

» An unmotivated High-C like Janet is probably concerned that she's being set up to make a mistake or fail. Or that the process is flawed somehow and will lead the whole group to disaster.
» This might cause her to feel slighted, in that no one bothered asking her to bring her expertise and insight to the conversation earlier in the process, when she might have prevented the problem.
» She might also believe that other people on the team have been assigned roles that don't particularly suit them. If someone in another role isn't detailed enough in the High-C's estimation, then the High-C often believes that nothing else matters because the project is screwed from the start.

How to Pitch a High-C (Conscientious)

» Push: "If we don't succeed in this project, people will say or think that you were wrong or incompetent. You're part of the team,

and if you give up and don't care, and the team makes a mistake, even if you're not responsible, you're guilty by association."
- » Pull: Appeal to their expertise. "We can't do this without your knowledge and experience."
- » The High-C's biggest fear is appearing to have failed at something. Keep that in mind to prove your point.
- » This profile will not be moved by any emotional, sappy appeal. In fact, the more emotional your story or plea is, the more they will be turned off.
- » Your motivation needs to be steeped in evidence. Now, you can share a story as evidence as long as it's relevant and points to facts. But use extreme caution with any story, because this profile hates salespeople and motivational talks.
- » In fact, this profile likes to poke holes in flippant comparisons and metaphors that are not precisely the same. So, any story you share should simply highlight a track-record of performance.
- » This profile likes to solve puzzles, so if time permits, ask them to investigate the situation and come back with an analysis. This will reinvigorate them and help commit them to the project. If there's no time for this type of analysis now, ask them to get through this particular project, and once it's completed, start the investigation.

Here's what all of this looks like in action:

BILL (LEADER)
Hi, Janet. Can we talk about those edits to the Swift language?

JANET (EMPLOYEE)
Sure.

BILL (LEADER)
[smiling] Look, we really can't get this done without you. There's no one else here

who knows the Apple iOS quite like you, and you're the only one who can code in Swift. We always appreciate your skillset, but if there was ever a time the team needed you, it's now.

JANET (EMPLOYEE)
[furrowing her brow] I'm already pushing up against my maximum consecutive hours here. Do you really think we can meet this deadline, even if I deliver?

BILL (LEADER)
I've seen you do tougher things before. Remember when you pulled us out of that fire with the data dump fiasco? You took 2,000 lines of code and analyzed it in half the time it'd take anyone else to do the same. Plus, you caught five serious flaws in the code that would have been a major disaster for the project.

JANET (EMPLOYEE)
[dispassionately] I remember.

BILL (LEADER)
In a lot of ways, your heroics on that piece is what made us all believe that we could meet this deadline. So, I'm sorry, but this whole thing is sort of a product of your own success.

JANET (EMPLOYEE)
Well then, maybe you need to pay me more. Or perhaps I should slow down.

BILL (LEADER)

Hahaha... Well, I tell you what, as much we need your expertise, I don't want it to work against you. So, here's what we could do. After we meet this deadline, I would like you to investigate and analyze why we keep finding ourselves in this situation. Maybe you can recommend rules or policies we might be able to put into place to prevent this type of fire drill from becoming the norm. In fact, I know you're crunched now, but perhaps there's a few top-of-mind things you can jot down now that are major red flags, and then you can dive into them next week.

JANET (EMPLOYEE)

Ummm... well, I can't promise anything. The next fire drill is already in the works.

BILL (LEADER)

And that's exactly the mistake we don't want to keep happening. For now, we need you to hit the Friday deadline. If we don't get there, we're going to have failed, and people are going to wonder why.

JANET (EMPLOYEE)

[pensively] But how do I know that Antonio and Paula will follow through on their end, even if I get this done somehow?

BILL (LEADER):

[presenting a report] They're already at the point where all they need is your edits and they're set. Whether we hit this deadline hinges on whether you can get your piece done.

JANET (EMPLOYEE)

[hesitantly] Okay. Well. Yeah, I'll see what I can do.

BILL (LEADER)

[departing] Thanks, Janet. Just let me know if you need anything.

THE WIN WITH A HIGH-C

- » The Win in this conversation comes from appealing to the High-C's expertise and proclivity for quality. Find ways to lean on her input and make her recognize how much you value that input, intellect, and excellence, and she will begin to become unstuck.
- » No lie: this will be the toughest person to motivate. Her natural disposition is that of skepticism. She doesn't like emotion. Even with data and proof, she might not look motivated. She will start moving only after she thinks about what you said (which will likely not be on the spot).
- » Don't expect her to say, "Son of a gun! You're right. I'm going to get going right now."
- » How she will respond: Think of your efforts with the High-C as planting seeds that will sprout later. You'll need to follow up with her (maybe many times) and say something like, "You've had some time to think about what I said. What do you think we should do?" Even then, she won't tell you that you were exactly right. She'll likely have more facts and details you'll have to address. But don't address these points. High-C profiles love to engage in theoretical debates, but there's probably no time for such debates right now. Simply defer to a later time when these points can be addressed.
- » How she will respond: She'll be a little "blah" about it. She won't be hugely expressive. Her motivation will be internal. And you'll need to keep after her.

THE PROFILES

D (DRIVER)

How to Approach a High-D

- » Avoid getting too deep into the details. Be short, to the point, and clear in your explanations. Making grand appeals to the greater needs of humanity won't get you anywhere with someone so results oriented.
- » This isn't because he doesn't care about humanity (heck, he might even *be* a humanitarian); it's because he feels stuck, stalled, treading water, and not sure how or if he'll ever get out. That feeling that there hasn't been any progress and there's no end to the struggle in sight is a sure way to demotivate a High-D.
- » Another sure way to demotivate a High-D is to bog him down in endless details—especially concerning work that he may feel is insignificant to the outcome. If it feels slow and stupid to the Driver, he will quickly lose motivation.
- » The best approach is to help the High-D see that action and progress are in fact happening, and that there has been positive movement forward. Or, show him how once he achieves this task, he can then quickly move on to other, bigger, more pressing matters.
- » It goes something like this: "I know it seems like you're not getting anywhere, but if you put in the hard work and time now, it'll catapult you to greater heights once we're done." In other words, patience is a difficult virtue for the Driver to accept, so you've got to show them how it's worth it.
- » It's okay to be a little more blunt with the language. If there is a profile that would be motivated by a kick in the pants, it's the Driver.
- » Make the ROI clearer, and you'll be well on your way to the Win.

How to Pitch a High-D

» Push: "If you don't do what we're asking of you, things are going to be harder, take longer, and cost us more money."
» Pull: "If you do what we're asking of you, you're going to get further and faster soon enough. The payout in terms of time or money will be significant. But we can't achieve the results if you don't put in the work now."
» When Pitching the Driver, keep in mind that they're always looking for a guarantee of results. For example, High-D executives don't go through the long and arduous process of MBA school because they love learning, but rather, because they know they will see a return from having those three powerful letters next to their name.

The Win with a High-D

» Expect him to say something crass: "Well, if those motherf@&*ers *really* knew what was going on here…"
» If you give him some immediate action he can take, or provide a clear next step to accomplish, then you'll start to see him chipping away and moving forward.
» How he will respond: you can expect quick action, but also a lot of attitude.

(INFLUENCER)

How to Approach a High-I

» If an Influencer is unmotivated, it's usually because her task isn't exciting enough for her. Maybe she sees that she isn't going to be personally recognized for this, or perhaps that her individual glory will be diminished.

- » Further, she might feel like there's not enough social interaction to make her tasks fun or interesting or important.
- » The surest way to demotivate a High-I is to stick her in a lab by herself and tell her to do 5,000 pages of solo work.

How to Pitch a High-I

- » Push: "Do you want people to think less of you? Do you want to be embarrassed? Do you want to be known for being lazy and not holding up your end of the bargain?"
- » Pull: "If anybody in this office can do this, it's *you*. When people see what you've done to carry this team, oh man, they might just write a book about you."
- » Notice the appeal to the ego, and to the desire for glory just for the individual.

The Win with a High-I

- » To achieve the Win with a High-I, you must demonstrate how this task will glorify her, and how much others will see her star shine brighter and higher in the sky for all to admire.
- » The High-I *loves* being motivated and inspired. If you can paint a rosy enough picture about how she is essential and how great she will be as a result, she will leave with a positive attitude and a promise to start moving.
- » The downside is that because she is so easily distracted, she will walk away feeling wonderful, but might not take action quickly. So, be sure to follow up with her very soon.
- » How she will respond: she'll be happy and motivated, but you will want to follow up to make sure she remains on task.

S (STABILIZER)

How to Approach a High-S

- » Typically, demotivation happens here because the Stabilizer is feeling like there's too much change and too much urgency. He is dedicated to his routines and "how things have always been done."
- » He might also feel like his territory is being impeded upon. He's very territorial. "This is my job, and someone's trying to take a portion of what I do away from me."
- » At the same time, the Stabilizer is rigorously dedicated to the sense of team. He could be unmotivated because he is perceiving that something is wrong with the team, or that not everyone is happy with the way things are being done. The High-S might even feel like repeated minor annoyances within a team are indicative of a crappy or poisonous work environment. Culture is very important to this profile.

How to Pitch a High-S

- » Push: "If you don't do this, you're going to cause heartache and headaches for the other people on the team. And the process is going to suffer as a result."
- » Pull: "If you do this, this will be a better and more caring workplace. The process will be much smoother. And the impact this will have on our customers' lives will be such an improvement for their careers and families."
- » Notice that in both cases, we're not appealing to the Stabilizer's singular sense of self, but rather to the glory of the team.

The Win with a High-S

- » The path to the Win with the Stabilizer is to demonstrate that you are aware of everyone's needs, and that work is in process to make sure everyone is satisfied. Further, you will want to show that the positive results far outweigh any perception of hostility and tension. Remember, this profile doesn't like conflict.

» This will be a long, drawn-out conversation. He'll be a little more emotional about it. "But don't you understand?" "Don't you see?"
» Lay out the next few steps in the process. Show him the full recipe and how it will all unfold. He needs to see the big picture. Otherwise, he will begin to feel demotivated, lost within a giant machine that's just churning.
» How he will respond: he will most likely agree to what you ask, and will start taking steps right away, but he will probably seem like he's in a somber mood with many uncertainties still front of mind.

DREADED CONVERSATION #4

SOMEONE EMBARRASSED THEMSELVES (OR THE COMPANY). HOW DO I MAKE SURE THEY NEVER DO IT AGAIN?

People screw up and do stupid things.

Whatever the nature of the screwup, and wherever it occurs, the bottom line is that it's not unheard of for even a star player to do something inappropriate, against company policy, or otherwise in violation of the code of conduct. Sometimes the greatest employees succumb to weakness, and in one huge mistake, manage to do something that jeopardizes their reputation and the organization's standing either internally or externally. The question isn't whether this will happen at some point (it absolutely will); the question is what is the best, most productive way to respond to these situations.

If you're part of a large organization with a robust HR staff, there's a good chance that you already have company policies that you can lean on to guide your way—although such policies don't automatically mean that it's going to be any less of a Dreaded Conversation. If you don't have any company policies in place, then you might really be reeling for solutions. Either way, this is one of the most difficult conversations a person can have in a professional setting. If you try to ignore it, you run the risk of it happening again. Perhaps worse, if you ignore it, you risk looking like an inept leader who plays favorites, tolerates reckless behavior, or is too incompetent to right a wrong.

So let's not be that type of leader!

THE CONVERSATION

PARTICIPANTS

» **SARA** is the leader of a sales team for a medical device company. She is excited about promoting the company's new defibrillator product at an upcoming showcase conference.
» **MARTY** is the top salesperson at the company. During the conference's opening night meet-and-greet, his drunken antics made him the unfortunate center of attention in front of coworkers, competitors, and even clients and prospects.

LOCATION

» Sara's office, following a morning in which the rumor mill is already running at full tilt

SARA (LEADER)

Marty, I understand there was an embarrassing incident last week at the conference. Somehow, I missed it, because I was busy entertaining other clients, but word got back to me before the night was even over. And I've been told that the embarrassment kind of hung over everyone's heads all week long.

MARTY (EMPLOYEE)

Yeah, I guess things maybe got a little out of hand. But you see, Darius from Bruxnor Inc.—you know Darius, I think...he's one of the first clients I brought into the company. Anyway, Darius and I have kind of a history of cutting loose a little at these functions. And you know, his wife is going through that medical issue and he just felt like tying on one of the defibrillator pads and having some fun. So, yeah, I guess—for the sake of one of my oldest and best clients—I had one or two more than I probably should have, and allowing our product to be part of that scene wasn't the best.

SARA (LEADER)

[gently] I guess I can see your perspective. But you have to understand that company policy expressly forbids disorderly conduct at any work function, particularly in front of clients and prospects.

MARTY (EMPLOYEE)

[very animated] Look, boss, I get it. And I can't tell you how sorry I am. I know that my behavior wasn't appropriate, and that I hurt some feelings and stepped on some toes. But I should also mention that Darius was there with Elaine from Stigman, and you know I've been trying to bring them on as a client almost since I started in this industry ten years ago. I've never really been able to get them to the table, though, you know? They're my white whale. And I finally had one of their reps listening at the bar, and I felt like the only way I could get Elaine to stick around was to keep Darius happy. And Darius seemed to want to drink. So I accommodated him. And you know what? I think I really made some progress with Elaine.

SARA (LEADER)

[meekly] As I understand it, Elaine left the two of you about a half-hour into the ordeal.

MARTY (EMPLOYEE)

Is that right? Well, no matter. You've seen me work. A half-hour is more than enough time for me to make an impression.

SARA (LEADER)

Well you certainly made an impression. That much is clear. Look, I know how these things happen. We've seen it all before. It's why there is a passage about the subject in the company rulebook. It's also why we met as a team on Friday to remind everyone to keep it under control at the function.

MARTY (EMPLOYEE)

[pleading] But you don't understand, I might get more business from two different companies because of this.

SARA (LEADER)

Of course that does matter. And, Marty, we absolutely value your contribution with this company. But the problem is that people are talking. Not just within our team, and not just within the company. We've already heard from several clients and prospects about the incident, and not in a positive light.

MARTY (EMPLOYEE)

[under his breath] Sounds like they need to lighten up.

SARA (LEADER)

[ignoring the comment] The folks in HR have passed along some information, along with this. [slides a form across his desk] We're issuing you this formal writeup. We need you to sign it. When it's signed, we'll be placing it in your employee profile.

MARTY (EMPLOYEE)

[signing without really reading] Yeah, yeah. Of course. Whatever you need to make this go away.

SARA (LEADER)

[gently] We're not just trying to make this go away. What we want is to be assured that this won't ever happen again.

MARTY (EMPLOYEE)

[holding his hand up in a pledge] I swear it won't ever happen again.

THE ANALYSIS

Sara is a High-S (Stabilizer)

Here is how we know:

- » She is somewhat indirect and non-confrontational.
- » She doesn't yell nor make any direct, personal attacks against Marty.
- » Her argument is based on the rulebook and not a personal affront.
- » You can sense some apprehension in her engagement.
- » She talked more about the image of the company and the team, and (unfortunately) accepted Marty's points about how he's been the company's rainmaker and should be allowed some leeway.

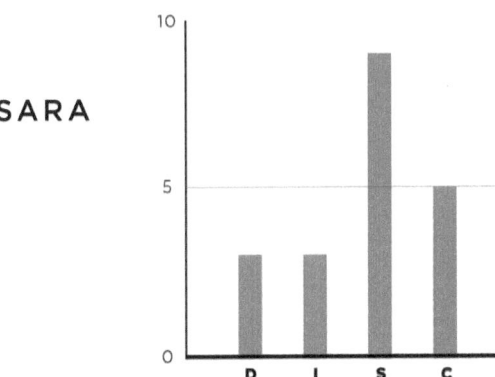

SARA

Marty is a High-I (Influencer)
with D (Driver) being a close second

- » His actions and behaviors were animated.
- » He proved eager to tell the story of how he got himself into the unfortunate situation.
- » The word "I" showed up repeatedly during his explanations about what happened and how he felt about the situation.
- » He implied several times that these clients wouldn't even be clients if not for him.
- » Marty doesn't seem too concerned with the rules. For him, it's more about the win.
- » He just wants to dismiss the incident and move forward.
- » When he departed, because Sara wasn't more assertive, he might have said he wouldn't allow this mistake to happen again, but we're not entirely sure that Marty will avoid repeating the behavior.

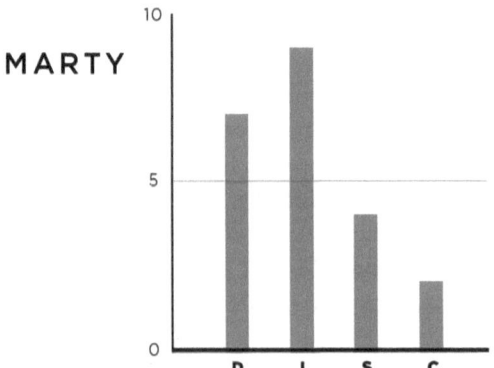

Sara held a "professional" conversation with Marty, but professional and productive are two very different concepts. Consider the general ineffectiveness of merely asking a person to sign a piece of paper promising never to screw up again. It goes back to what I wrote at the start of this chapter. People screw up. It happens. Asking them to sign a piece of paper that merely says "I'll never screw up again" is pretty preposterous when you think about it. It's like asking them to sign a paper that says, "I'll cease being human in the future."

In situations like these, if we're going to get people to overcome the lesser parts of their human nature, then we don't need demerits; we need *reinforcements of the message*. We get that by compelling the offending party to do something that makes him a little uncomfortable. Why? Because it isn't the initial embarrassing behavior that sticks with most offenders, it is the *discomfort* and *embarrassment* that follows.

If we know the offending party's unique performance profile, then we can find ways to lean on all those things that make them a little uncomfortable. This way, we communicate to them—clearly and effectively—that we don't take this situation lightly, it's a serious offense, and it absolutely cannot happen again. As a bonus, such situations can be used to further reinforce the far-reaching consequences not just to the offending employee, but to other people in the company as well.

PERFORMANCE PRINCIPLE

THE APOLOGY TOUR

So if a writeup isn't effective enough, what do you do? How do you make sure this person doesn't just shrug it off and go back to the same behaviors once the heat dies down? It starts by requiring him to apologize to everyone he has offended, and in a way that plays against the offending party's profile—particularly to make it uncomfortable.

Wait? An apology tour? Really? Yes, really. There are three good reasons why requiring employees to apologize is far more effective than simply writing them up:

1. An apology tour forces the offender to revisit his embarrassing behavior in the refreshing, reflective light of repentance (even if the repenting is an assignment from the boss).
2. An apology tour helps mend wounds that *other people* may have suffered as a result of this behavior. It allows other key players to know that the offending party recognizes his mistakes, realizes how it made the other key players feel, and is contrite and genuine in his promise that it will never happen again.

3. It helps quash the rumor mill. In these situations, the rumors can be just as damaging as the actual event. Direct apologies allow the offending party to tell the story straight, which silences the whispers, ends the confusion, and puts the conversation to bed almost immediately.

The above is true, provided we keep three caveats in mind:

1. There is no one-size-fits all. Depending on the situation, it may be more appropriate for you to request that the offending party host the apology tour in an open conference room. Perhaps this person is such a problem employee that you don't feel comfortable allowing him to meet with another employee in a closed office. There are no hard-and-fast rules here. The apologies can happen anywhere, so long as they happen in an open, honest, and above all, safe way.
2. Not *all* mistakes require an apology tour. The situations we're covering are those that could ultimately be damaging to the company.
3. It's not enough just to say, "Bob, you need to go around and tell everyone you're sorry." Some profiles don't mind a quick, less-than-heartfelt apology. For others, that kind of thing is about as ineffective as a protocol-following writeup. This is why we need to dictate the terms of the apology a little more. It's not enough to just say you're sorry. You must also require the offending party to speak to those he offended about topics that will make him a little uncomfortable. The harder it is for him to do this, the less likely he will be to repeat the behavior.

SAY THIS!

Since Marty's profile is High-I, let's first examine the Approach, Pitch, and Win associated with a more effective conversation with an Influencer. As I mentioned, the Approach in this specific Dreaded Conversation is all about leaning on what each profile doesn't *like*.

How to Approach a High-I (Influencer)

» High-I's don't like:
  › To be embarrassed
  › To think that her status or image has diminished in the eyes of the company or her peers
  › To believe that people don't like her anymore

How to Pitch the High-I (Influencer)

» Since Marty is an Influencer, let's take a look at a better way to Pitch him.

> **YOU (LEADER)**
> Marty, you see that I've invited Donna from HR to join us, and I think you know why. We've all heard the story from any number of different people. Now I'd like to hear it from you.

Note: Marty will go on and on about his side of the story and will offer great detail on exactly how he found himself in that situation. Let him talk. It's the only way to get him to fully appreciate the many facets of the mistake he made.

> **YOU (LEADER)**
> [patiently] I understand. I also understand that this company needs you. You're a top performer, and in many ways, the face of our salesforce.

> **MARTY (EMPLOYEE)**
> [contrite] I appreciate that, boss.

YOU (LEADER)
This is exactly why this writeup Donna has brought for you to sign isn't enough. The fact that you're so high-profile means we have to take action to ensure that this never happens again.

MARTY (EMPLOYEE)
[very animated] I'll do whatever it takes to put this behind me.

YOU (LEADER)
[firmly] When we're done here, I want you to spend the rest of the morning visiting [list the head of each team that was impacted by Marty's behavior, followed by the names of every coworker who you believe has been embarrassed or otherwise hindered by what happened]. You're going to apologize to each of them individually. Then, we're going to gather your whole team together and you're going to apologize to them, as well.

MARTY (EMPLOYEE)
[looking a little less enthusiastic] Of course.

YOU (LEADER)
[firmly] I have to stress that I'm not looking for just an "I'm sorry." I want you to apologize to everyone by explaining to them exactly how embarrassed you are, and how you understand that you have embarrassed them as well. I want you to highlight all the ways that this behavior has hurt the company and diminished us in the eyes of our clients and our competition. And I

> want you to specifically itemize at least three separate things about the incident that you did that were examples of inappropriate and embarrassing behavior.
>
> Please understand that I'm not doing this because I'm just trying to put you through the wringer. I also want to fix the damage you've done. And I want to make sure that people stop gossiping, because if the rumors continue, I'm afraid it won't only hurt the company. There are people here who just won't like you anymore.

However you deliver the message, the key points to hit are the ones that play against Marty's aversions.

- » To make that apology really uncomfortable for him (something he won't soon forget), the angle to take is to have him talk about how his mistake looks bad for the company and how it diminishes his image, credibility, accomplishments, and achievements.
- » Insist that he return to you after completing the apology tour to debrief what he said, who he said it to, and what others may have said back to him. This is also a bit of an accountability step that ensures he followed through with the apologies and positioned them the way you wanted.
- » Important Note: Again, be sure to put a timestamp on the point when he must complete the apology tour. This is something that needs to be addressed sooner rather than later.

The Win with a High-I (Influencer)

- » When this profile returns to debrief you on his apology tour, he will share stories and feedback about what people might have said in response, and perhaps details about various expressions and reactions from coworkers. He might even recite verbatim

what was said in each apology meeting. Just let him talk (up to a point), because talking is therapeutic for a High-I.
» When he is finished, give some positive reinforcement. "You are the personification of our brand. People associate you with the face of this organization. I don't need someone creating treason when they're supposed to be an ambassador."
» Whatever your approach, it's always best to look back into the track record at times when the High-I did well. Then, close by reminding that we don't need these distractions in the future.

THE PROFILES

D (DRIVER)

How to Approach a High-D

» The High-D doesn't like:
  › Showing sensitivity or describing feelings (theirs or other people's)
  › Supposedly "pointless" efforts that take up a lot of their time
  › Looking like they're wasting resources, have caused themselves or the company to lose money/profits, or have caused production or impact to slow down
» So, use these natural dislikes of the High-D profile against itself.

How to Pitch a High-D

» It is a good idea to require a larger number of apologies than you might normally. This helps play against her natural aversion to tasks that feel like they're too time consuming and unproductive. In this situation, the more groups you send her to apologize to, the more it will sting, and the deeper the message will sink in.

- » Tell her to admit to each person that she wasn't thinking clearly of how her actions impacted the company, and how those actions could cost the company money, productivity, and getting further ahead with customers.
- » More directly, instruct the High-D that on this apology tour she must share how this embarrassing situation makes her feel, and then she must also ask each person receiving the apology how it made them feel. The central goal here is to put the High-D in a series of situations where she must discuss emotions—something that will make her uncomfortable.
- » Insist that she return to you after completing the apology tour to debrief.
- » Important Note: Be sure to put a timestamp on the point when she must complete the apology tour. This is something that needs to be addressed sooner rather than later.

THE WIN WITH A HIGH-D

- » During the post-apology tour debrief, she will be short, blunt, and will want to move on. You won't see many signs of remorse. She won't share further emotional detail. Expect her to say something like, "Okay, that's done. Let's move on."
- » To reinforce the message, you will want to say something like "You're a producer in this business. I need you producing and focused." The goal will be to encourage, remind her of her value, and reinforce the idea that behaviors like these only serve to slow us down and damage our bottom line.

S (STABILIZER)

How to Approach a High-S

- » The High-S doesn't like:
  - › Conflict
  - › Tension
  - › Heartaches and headaches (for himself or for the team/company)
  - › The thought that there is dissent among the team as a result of his actions

How to Pitch a High-S

- » The High-S's apology should focus on how his actions caused other people to feel awkward or embarrassed.
- » In the High-S's apologies, he should have to admit to how the mistake has caused political fallout with a wide scope, and dysfunction for the team and company.
- » He needs to point out that now the competitors might be able to use this against the company, so it'll have far-reaching team and business impact. Then, ask him to apologize for causing this to happen.
- » The apology must include how the actions of one person have now caused headaches, heartaches, and much-needed crisis control for so many others.
- » Insist that he return to you after completing the apology tour to debrief.
- » Important Note: Be sure to put a timestamp on the point when he must complete the apology tour. This is something that needs to be addressed sooner rather than later.

The Win with a High-S

- » At the debrief session, the High-S will be apologetic, but in a much less animated way compared to the High-I. He will probably not share a lot of stories, because he doesn't want to keep this conflict and tension persisting.

» You should follow up with, "You are the embodiment of teamwork and organization. You're the hinge and the go-between for so many groups in this organization. You've helped us develop systems and processes, and you always make sure people feel engaged. What I don't need is my catalyst for engagement being disengaged with a stupid action."

 **(CONSCIENTIOUS)**

How to Approach a High-C

» The High-C doesn't like:
  › Thinking she is wrong
  › The idea that other people believe she made a mistake
  › The accusation that her actions were illogical, or that she didn't think before acting
  › The idea that she created evidence that can be used to damage the company
  › Emotions and sensitivity

How to Pitch a High-C

» Out of all the profiles, the High-C will be most uncomfortable with having to give an apology.
» In her apology tour, tell this profile to:
  › Admit to making a mistake. In fact, insist that each apology include the words, "I made a big mistake."
  › Show evidence of how the mistake might impact the team or company.
  › Apologize for illogical behavior and not thinking before she acted.
  › Describe the unpleasant emotions she stirred up for others

and how they are probably feeling now about the collateral damage due to her sophomoric actions.
- » Insist that she return to you after completing the apology tour to debrief.
- » **Important Note**: Be sure to put a timestamp on the point when she must complete the apology tour. This is something that needs to be addressed sooner rather than later.

The Win with a High-C

- » At the post-apology debrief, the High-C will be about as straightforward as they come. "That's done," she will say.
- » Expect a little sulkiness. Apologies and admitting wrong hurts the most for this profile. She isn't likely to thank you for it or apologize any further.
- » Reinforce the message with, "You are one of the best critical thinkers in this organization. Your expertise is proven, and a source of pride for all of us. Don't let something stupid undermine all the hard work and experience you provide us with each day."

DREADED CONVERSATION #5

I DON'T GET ALONG WITH THIS PERSON. HOW DO I LEAD THEM?

Before we start, let's get one thing clear: this chapter isn't going to make you friends with every single person at work. What it *will* do is show you how to resonate and connect with the people that you absolutely have to get along with if you're going to advance the relationship, help the team, and be productive. Think about it like this: you have to lead someone who is nothing at all like you. In a social setting, there is no way you're going to be friends. But for this project to succeed, you have to make sure everyone works well together. This chapter will show you how to do that.

THE CONVERSATION

Participants

- » **MALORY** has grown into the role of lead architect for her firm, though she is not one of its four founders.
  - › This isn't the first time Malory has had to approach Lindsey with a disagreement about a design choice, and she is beginning to grow annoyed about how her persistent points don't seem to be sinking in with Lindsey.
- » **LINDSEY** is an interior designer for the firm's full-service clients.

- › She used to run her own interior design company prior to being acquired by the firm. Her role with the firm is somewhat new, but her skills are quickly helping take her employer to the next level.

Location

- » Lindsey's office
    - › Lindsey prefers to keep her desk in the more open space of the office, along with the rest of her team.
    - › Fortunately, Malory has chosen to bring this conversation up to Lindsey while the rest of her team is at lunch—though they are certainly not alone in the open-office floorplan.

MALORY (LEADER)

[in a huff] Lindsey, we've got to review these furniture and color choices you just submitted.

LINDSEY (EMPLOYEE)

[ignoring Malory's tone] Yeah, I'm loving that lime green. I think it'll really boost productivity for the client's creative staff. It might cost a little more to go with that supplier, but the ROI will be worth it almost immediately.

MALORY (LEADER)

[focusing on the drawings she has brought] Listen, no. That's fine. The color is beside the point. Although, while we're on the subject, like I've been telling you, the client isn't going to love how the green clashes with their logo. Did you see the latest white paper I wrote and published on Color Continuity? Make sure you read that. Also, here's the document of client-requested specs. Let's go through it, shall we?

Five minutes of explanation pass.

> But the more important point is back at the top of the page. You see what we have there at the top? It says they want an open floor plan just like ours.
>
> **LINDSEY** (EMPLOYEE)
> [not bothering to look] Yes, yes. An open and flowing space. You've been very thorough. And anyway, you showed me all these details last time.
>
> **MALORY** (LEADER)
> [annoyed] Then maybe you can tell me how this filing system you're suggesting we place between their development and sales team pods helps meet the need for open and flowing space.
>
> **LINDSEY** (EMPLOYEE)
> They're *open* shelves. You can see through them to the other side. The sky-blue liners will offset the green in a way that pops. It's a really striking feature.
>
> **MALORY** (LEADER)
> You can see through them?
>
> **LINDSEY** (EMPLOYEE)
> Yes.
>
> **MALORY** (LEADER)
> Can you *walk* through them? No. So, it doesn't meet the spec. It's wrong.
>
> **LINDSEY** (EMPLOYEE)
> [shaking her head, annoyed] ...

MALORY (LEADER)

[turning to leave] That means it doesn't fit *open* space planning. Now, change it.

LINDSEY (EMPLOYEE)

[sighing] Whatever you say, boss.

MALORY (LEADER)

[returning to the desk to leave the list] I'll just leave this here so we don't overlook any more details.

THE ANALYSIS

Malory is a High-C (conscientious)

Here's how we know:

- » She presented evidence in the form of her newly published white paper and then led a five-minute conversation about the client's spec list.
- » She was quick to annoyance about Lindsey's somewhat dismissive attitude related to the details.
- » She used condescending sarcasm to make her point about the see-through filing system.

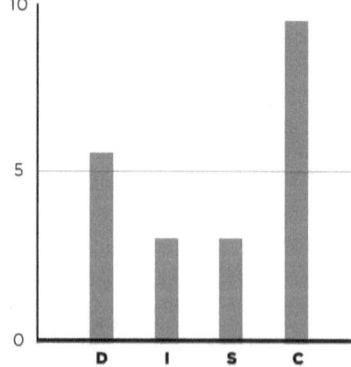

Lindsey is a High-D (Driver)
with I (Influencer) being a close second

» She talked in terms of expense and ROI right out of the gate.
» She was less interested in drilling down on the details.
» She seemed more interested in results and getting the project done than in bothering to review the list.
» She seemed rather excited about the lime green color scheme she'd submitted (this is the hint of her second-place I-profile).

LINDSEY

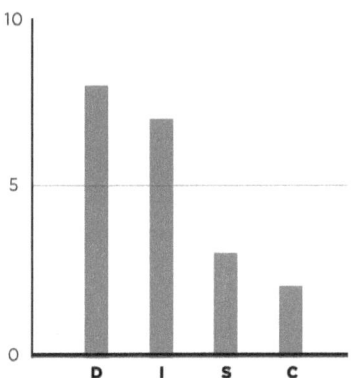

PERFORMANCE PRINCIPLE

A World of Self-Interest

There's a Dale Carnegie principle that says, "Talk in terms of the other person's interests." This is a really good, incredibly useful principle—particularly in a professional setting—because it takes the focus off you and puts it on the other person.

A couple hundred years ago, famed economist Adam Smith wrote something reminiscent of this point, but more recently, a client and good friend of mine, Jim Scalo, put it succinctly. "We live in a world of self-interest." Jim is a tremendously successful entrepreneur and owner of Burns Scalo Real Estate, a commercial real estate business in Pittsburgh, PA. He has always been incredibly well plugged in to the cultural side of people development, and he is one of the most authentic and effective leaders you'd meet.

So what are Mr. Carnegie, Mr. Smith, and Mr. Scalo talking about here? Well, some people might say that they don't like talking about themselves (and depending on their profile, that can absolutely be true), but that doesn't mean they aren't still self-interested. Yes, while some people might not like talking about themselves, *everyone* loves hearing about things that are tailored to their interests.

The trick is figuring out what those things are. So, while Dale Carnegie's principle is brilliant, it is also too broad. Fortunately, DISC allows us to narrow this broad principle into more specific terms and interests.

Additionally, the goal isn't just to talk about *what* you think the other person may like, but also to talk about it in the specific *way* that they will want to hear it. For instance, we know that a High-D like Lindsey prefers to talk mostly about results, but if you start trying to talk about *how* we're going to get those results, you're going to lose her. The message is important, yes, but the *style* with which you deliver the message is even more so. It's not what you say, but how you say it, right?

SAY THIS!

How to Approach a High-D (Driver)

» The Driver is a conqueror. She likes to hear about her accomplishments.
» She also likes to lead, so let her lead.
» Conversely, if she's in a subordinate role, then the Approach will be to give her clear motivation (but not necessarily specific direction) to achieve the results we're after. In other words, create a role that allows her to win and conquer on her own terms.
» Give her an outcome to achieve and then get out of her way so she can achieve it.
» Remember to share the specific results we're looking for. She's interested in money and profit. She wants ROI.

How to Pitch a High-D (Driver)

- » When you're the boss of a High-D, it's best to lead her in the direction you want her to go while also sounding like you're in command. The Driver is indeed a *driver* and will respond much more favorably to tasks that feel both self-directed and worth her investment in time and energy. So, coming across as unsure or hesitant will only frustrate and annoy the High-D.
- » Keep in mind, though, that if you're *not* the Driver's boss (whether you're her equal or subordinate), the opposite is true. In these situations, it is best to allow the High-D to feel in command.
- » In all cases, keep the conversation short. Don't pontificate. Remember, the Driver operates best when she is getting things done.
- » When you're in the conversation, talk about how you're going to knock this out of the park, and you're going to do it quickly. ("This is going to be big league. The best anyone has ever seen. And we're going to get it done on time and under budget. This is going to be an easy win.")
- » Discuss the big picture. It should all be about ROI—money, winning, efficiency, accomplishment, and so on. If appropriate, it's fine to hint at advancing her career and potential for a bonus.

Here's what all of that looks like in the context of our mock conversation from above:

YOU (LEADER)
[directly] Lindsey, I have some concerns about a couple of these furniture and color choices you've submitted.

LINDSEY (EMPLOYEE)
Yeah, I'm loving that lime green. I think it'll really boost productivity for their creative staff. It might cost a little more to go with that supplier, but the ROI will be worth it almost immediately.

YOU (LEADER)

[agreeably] Good points, but the client asked us to keep it simple and stay on brand with the colors. Plus, they're looking to maximize the effect and usage of the open space. That extends to interior design.

LINDSEY (EMPLOYEE)

What are you suggesting?

YOU (LEADER)

[direct] We want light and airy. We have to use the plans we've drawn to their maximum potential. This means we can't have furniture cluttering up the open sightlines.

LINDSEY (EMPLOYEE)

Those are *open* shelves. You can see through them to the other side. The sky-blue liners will offset the green in a way that pops. It's a really striking feature.

YOU (LEADER)

That's true, but the two teams that are going to be on opposite sides of that shelving unit need lots of face-to-face interaction. If they have to walk around that barrier every time they need to talk or hand off a document, the client will lose efficiency.

LINDSEY (EMPLOYEE)

I guess I can see that.

YOU (LEADER)

So here's what I'd like you to do. Keep the color scheme simple and straightforward while also connecting it to the client's branding. And figure out a way to keep this great shelving unit without blocking the flow of movement between these two teams.

LINDSEY (EMPLOYEE)

[nodding] I guess I can do that.

YOU (LEADER)

I know I'm basically asking you to square-one this, but it's going to be worth it—fewer change orders and time delays on the back end. You'll knock it out of the park, and it's really going to sell this plan and move the project forward. And, hey, if they like the design on this floorplate, I'm betting they decide to go in with us on the executive office designs too. That'll be more work for your team, and it'll also provide more cases that the firm can use to pitch these services to future clients. It might sound like a lot of busywork, but it will take this relationship and this company to the next level.

LINDSEY (EMPLOYEE)

All right. I'm on it.

YOU (LEADER)

Thanks, Lindsey. This will all be worth it. It's going to be a great win!

The Win with a High-D (driver)

» The response from the High-D will be short and direct ("We'll get it done," she will say).

- » She might have alternative suggestions and might even challenge you about the deadline. This isn't a negative reaction. For a High-D, everything is a competition. Often, when she reacts this way, it's just because she likes egging people on.
- » The High-D won't be secretive about her endorsement or support of the idea, but you may need to follow up, because attention to detail isn't her strong suit.

THE PROFILES

 **(INFLUENCER)**

How to Approach a High-I

- » Gloat and dote on him. If you want him to like you, you have to show him that you like him too (because he really wants to be liked).
- » Encourage him to do all the talking.
- » Highlight how he can become the superstar.
- » The High-I is interested in status and image and recognition (either for himself or global recognition for the team he leads or company he owns).

How to Pitch a High-I

- » Echo the High-I's natural tendency for excitement. ("This will be such an exciting project. It'll revolutionize the way we do things! This is going to change the company!")
- » When it's time to talk about what needs to get done, be sure to emphasize the starring role the High-I will play. ("How about you take the first phase of this project, because you always win people over? That's a tough negotiation process there, and you're good with people and could really shine with this.")

» Don't forget to motivate him with the timeframe and a subtle reminder of how falling short of the mark will make him look bad. ("Problem is, we're going to need to get this done by two weeks from now. Otherwise, we'll wind up with egg on our face and people will think we don't know what we're doing.")

THE WIN WITH A HIGH-I

» The High-I will look and sound excited. He will be something of a cheerleader for the project.
» Expect him to be all in.
» If you've impressed him to the point of friendship, you'll get a good sense immediately about where you stand.
» If you're still feeling some resistance, just talk more about him. Ask questions that allow him to shine the spotlight on his own talents, skills, and accomplishments.
» Similar to the D profile, details are not a natural strength of the High-I profile. Stay on top of this person. They easily lose focus and get distracted.

S (STABILIZER)

HOW TO APPROACH A HIGH-S

» Make her feel supported and cared for. Be less direct and more cautious.
» Be sympathetic, caring, and concerned for her time, schedule, and conflicts. Changes in priority are challenges for her. So, find an agreed-upon time and take things a little slower.
» The High-S is interested in pleasing other people while also ensuring that everyone feels connected to the project and the people working on it. She wants to get things done in an orderly fashion and on schedule.

How to Pitch a High-S

» Slow things down. Stick to procedure. And always be aware of her feelings.
» Whenever you're done making a suggestion, be sure to use this key phrase: "Those are my thoughts, but how do you feel?" That's what the High-S wants to hear.
» The sense that you want to give the High-S during your pitch is that this is a team effort. You're not just telling her what to do; you're working together on this.
» If she seems to be getting lost in the details, then suggest some scheduling. "Let's get together and plan out these steps to revise this floorplate by Friday. In our meeting, let's bring our calendars, because I know we both have some other things going on and I want to be respectful of our time. So let's make sure we not only plan this out from start to finish, but we also give ourselves enough time to do this."
» On top of this, she is likely to respond favorably to the idea of involving a team approach. "We should collaborate with as many people as we can to make sure we do this right."

The Win with a High-S

» The High-S's facial expressions probably won't indicate that everything is completely copacetic between you. She will be more poker faced, and that's okay.
» She will be most concerned about getting something on the schedule soon and will probably pull out the schedule right away.
» Ironically, while this profile is list- and process-oriented, they are also highly challenged by prioritizing their actions. You can be supportive by helping them prioritize and schedule their approach to tasks. ("We need to do this first and then this and then this last. And let's also make sure this is decided by no later than the 15th of the month.")
» Show them the process and the way forward. Lay it out!

 **(CONSCIENTIOUS)**

How to Approach a High-C

» Be more direct, more business-minded.
» He wants to be around people he believes are smart and experts in their fields, so it's best to focus your conversations more on quality and intellectual thought.
» He's looking for someone with exacting standards, someone who is about quality and precision, and someone who shares his affinity for analysis.
» He doesn't mind debate, and loves launching into deep theoretical discussions of concepts. If you have theories of your own and don't mind engaging in a little benign mental sparring, it will certainly pique this profile's intellectual fancy. However, if you're not as deep of a theoretical thinker as the High-C, that's okay. You can still ask a question that provides the High-C an open forum to pontificate (and then just nod your head as you "consider his points").
» If and when you have to challenge his domain, be highly strategic and diplomatic about how to approach it. A full-frontal assault is never the answer. The words, "You're wrong" should never come out of your mouth when engaging a High-C. Such words are a personal attack to their very existence. Instead, you'll need to lay out the evidence and subtly imply that their thinking on this particular matter may not be the most correct.

How to Pitch a High-C

» The conversation should focus on quality and precision. ("We have to make sure that we include all the specifications they're asking for on this project, and I think there are some areas here that we can further improve upon in our proposal.")

- » Reference his sense of accomplishment. ("Your past projects have always been of phenomenal quality, so your input and expertise are really valuable in this area.")
- » Throw in a subtle appeal to his vanity. ("I know you won the award for technical construction last year. So I think just based on that, we can incorporate some of your ideas that will really wow the client.")
- » If there's a deadline, reference the timeframe, but build that reference around the dire need for his expertise. ("We need to have this proposal together in two weeks. Having some sketches or photos from those past projects of yours by next week would be helpful. Without them, the proposal isn't going to be as precise or exceptional as it could be.")
- » Use evidence (not emotion) to sell your points with this profile. The High-C doesn't care so much about how you feel or what you believe. Rather, he cares more about what you can prove.

The Win with a High-C

- » The High-C is likely to push back a little. He is either going to add to the evidence you suggested or criticize it. The key is not to take the criticism personally. Remember, his beef isn't with you. It's with the quality of the work product.
- » He likes people who talk about technical and intellectual things. As long as you're not at odds with him and saying directly that he is wrong, you're going to ingratiate yourself.
- » If he spars with you, that doesn't mean he doesn't like you. He just likes debate. Believe it or not, the more he debates you (assuming it's constructive), the more he likes you.

DREADED CONVERSATION #6

SOMEONE WANTS TO PURSUE A REALLY BAD IDEA. HOW DO I CHANGE THEIR MIND?

The focus of this chapter might sound kind of devious, but I promise it's all above board. There are times when another team member or leader would like to pursue something that (in your fully honest experience) just *isn't* going to work. With this chapter, we'll examine how to dissuade that person from pursuing a bad idea by using her performance profile against itself. A leader's job is to grow themselves, grow their team, and grow their company, so we're going to learn how to do that and still say no without looking like you're the hindrance, the "problem person," or the "naysayer" standing in the way of change and opportunity.

Again, we're not trying to manipulate anyone here. We just want to tell them what their profile needs to hear in order to wake them up and dissuade them from this bad decision. You know those scenes in the movies where someone slaps another person in the face and says, "Snap out of it!" Well, that's what we're trying to do here (minus the slapping).

THE CONVERSATION

PARTICIPANTS

» **JAMES**, the COO of an insurance company. He's the guy with a bad idea.

» **DEBORA**, the company's CTO. She needs to talk John out of his bad idea.

Location

» The boardroom. It's an impressive, modern space separated into a private wing of the building, so at least the only people who see and hear this conversation are in the c-suite.
» There are, however, four other executives in the room besides James and Debora.

JAMES (CO-WORKER)
[excitedly] I know we're all anxious to wrap up this meeting, but I did have one more idea on how to add a little more cohesion to all these new staffers we've hired this month.

DEBORA (LEADER)
[skeptically] You don't think they'll bond naturally over the shared work? Because in past hiring waves, that's always how it's happened. We've never had any trouble.

JAMES (CO-WORKER)
[grinning] I know, I know. But there's nothing wrong with a little help in teambuilding. I just think it would be good for everyone— not just in tech, but in the whole company— if we also work together on something that isn't work-related.

DEBORA (LEADER)
[definitely not grinning] Let's hear it then.

JAMES (CO-WORKER)
[somehow grinning bigger] Since we're now well into the fall season and all the holidays are around the corner, I'm thinking we do a bake sale!

DEBORA (LEADER)
[somehow grinning even less than before] I'm sorry? What?

JAMES (CO-WORKER)
Look, we've got fifteen different teambuilding exercises built into the employee onboarding program, and those are all great. There's no questioning that our new hire system works. But we need to hit the ground running heading into Q1, so let's do something fun that will really gel these new hires together.

DEBORA (LEADER)
But like you said, our onboarding process already *works*. All of our data on engagement and teamwork supports it and shows our ramp-up time is less than ninety-days.

JAMES (CO-WORKER)
No one's doubting that, Deb. We all appreciate how effective your training programs have been. I just think we could take advantage of the holidays coming up to really kick the cultural cohesion effort into high gear. We could have the culture committee send out an invite for a baking contest for Halloween, and—

DEBORA (LEADER)

[interrupting] Halloween! That's next week, James. Even if we get an invite out tomorrow, that gives these new hires just one weekend to arrange everything. You don't think they have enough on their plates already?

JAMES (CO-WORKER)

[losing steam] Well then, we stress that this first one is optional. And we could also promote future bake sales for Thanksgiving and Christmas. That gives people more time to plan. And we could rotate the charity that it benefits. I really think this will be fun. And it will give everyone an opportunity to show their talents to the other new hires—talents that aren't work related.

Everyone sort of lets the tension hang in the air for a while as James looks to the others for support and Debora cradles her head in her hands. Finally, she looks up.

DEBORA (LEADER)

Look. This just isn't going to work. At all. You're wrong. The new hires aren't here for crafts and cookies. They're here to learn how to do their jobs as efficiently as possible.

JAMES (CO-WORKER)

[poker faced] Well if you don't think it'll work...

DEBORA (LEADER)

[condescendingly] I don't. With all respect,

it's just not even in the ballpark of what anyone will want. Plus, it's trying to solve an issue that doesn't exist. The numbers don't lie. Every quarter for three years, we've brought in twenty new tech staffers. And the training has gotten them up to peak performance by the subsequent quarter every time. We don't need this. It's just a distraction.

JAMES (CO-WORKER)

Well then, I guess the nays have it. You know, this is the fourth culture improvement idea I've brought to the table over the last year that has automatically gotten shot down by this group. Apparently, that's the type of company culture you all want to have: all about business. It's clear that any new ideas about improving our culture and teambuilding process are just bad ideas. I think we can adjourn the meeting.

James leaves the meeting feeling belittled, berated, and insulted on an intellectual level. In short, he's hurt.

THE ANALYSIS

JAMES IS A HIGH-S (STABILIZER)

Here's how we know:

- » He's all about teambuilding.
- » The concept he brought to the table was meant to benefit everyone in a way that would enhance corporate culture.
- » When Debora started challenging him, he continued with long-winded explanations about why this would benefit others.

- » When it became clear that he wasn't going to win the debate, he quickly retreated.
- » He was obviously upset—albeit in a controlled and professional manner. Notice that when the conversation got a little hot, he didn't get *hysterical*, but he did get *historical* by citing past occasions.

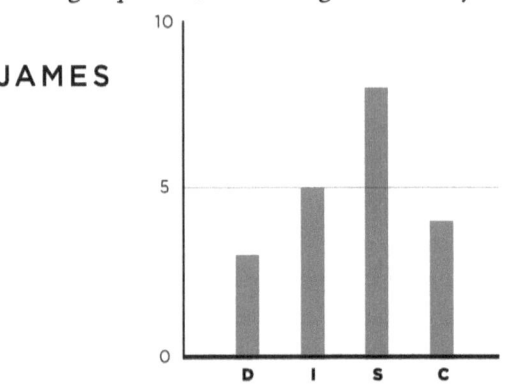

DEBORA IS A HIGH-C (CONSCIENTIOUS)

- » On more than one occasion, she referenced the data to support her argument.
- » She didn't mind being a little condescending.
- » She had trouble accepting an idea that wasn't her own (particularly since there was clearly nothing more than a gut feeling to back up the plan's efficacy).
- » Her responses flatly refused to acknowledge the benefit of anything that didn't adhere to the rigorous system she built.

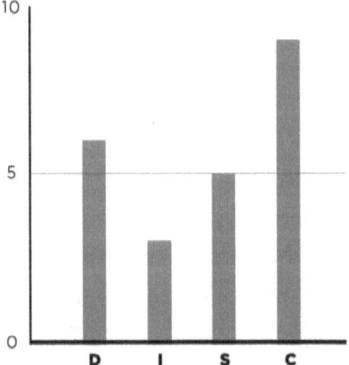

PERFORMANCE PRINCIPLE

Oh No vs. Let's Go

There are times when you have to dissuade someone from doing something that isn't going to be good. But you risk your dissention coming across as the *hurdle* to getting something done. You look like you're not a team player. Like you're a naysayer. Like you're the problem.

We don't want that. Here's what we do want: To use the DISC techniques with a mindset and leadership style of "let's go" rather than "oh no." Too often, the leaders I have encountered (especially the S's and C's, who are more technically driven) fall more into the latter camp.

Now, there is a caveat. I'm not suggesting that you need to pursue *every* opportunity someone proposes. This is a chapter about dissuading from bad ideas, after all. What I'm suggesting is that the mindset when you first approach the situation should always be, "Let's look into this and explore it," instead of, "Oh no, that won't work" from the get-go.

If you're someone (and I'm talking specifically to the D and C profiles now) who tends to quickly and bluntly discourage people's ideas, then you are conditioning your team not to think and problem-solve to their potential. Whereas a "Let's go" approach promotes a culture where ideas are explored and innovation is encouraged. Yes, of course, there are a lot of bad ideas you have to sift through in order to find those few good ideas. But you'll never find the good ones if you've conditioned people to stop pitching ideas from the start. So let's avoid the "oh no" leadership mindset and focus more on the "let's go" approach that moves people and ideas forward.

SAY THIS!

So here we are, having examined and explored the situation. We've checked the facts and evidence and listened with attentive ears. And after all that, we know very well that this is a genuinely bad idea. How do we dissuade the other person from pursuing it? More importantly, how do we dissuade them while still looking like we're in that "let's go" mindset?

Since James's profile is a Stabilizer, let's first examine the Approach, Pitch, and Win associated with a more effective conversation with a High-S.

How to Approach a High-S (Stabilizer)

- » When a High-S has an idea, he's going to come at it by covering all the bases. He's going to have laid out the process.
- » This will be a lengthy conversation.
- » He will probably promote a message that sounds completely altruistic. "Let's do this because it'll be so much better and help so many other people." James, for example, didn't want to do a bake sale because he just loves baking; he was in on this idea because he thought it would build stronger teams and raise money for charity.
- » The Stabilizer really wants to help the team. Although he is process oriented, he may not have thought through all the business implications and logistics.
- » He will be receptive to your no, but only if you do it gently. You can't yell at a Stabilizer and expect him to accept it and still be productive.

How to Pitch a High-S (Stabilizer)

- » It's best to play to the High-S's biggest fears, which include change and urgency. Convince him that if we pursue this idea, it's going to have a ripple effect that will cause heartaches and headaches for a lot of people.
- » We're not lying, of course. The case we make has to be genuine and honest. But if we position it so that this is a great idea that we should probably revisit next month, then we successfully redirect the Stabilizer.
- » Stabilizers like slow, methodical, no-pressure approaches. The goal is to position that this idea will be better served if we try it when we're *not* facing pressure or a tight deadline.

Here's what all of that looks like:

> **JAMES** (CO-WORKER)
> [excitedly] I know we're all anxious to wrap up this meeting, but I did have one more idea on how to add a little more cohesion to all these new technology staffers we had to bring in this month.
>
> **YOU** (LEADER)
> [patiently] Let's hear it.
>
> **JAMES** (CO-WORKER)
> [grinning] We've seen in the past how non-work-related activities can build bonds and make teams more effective. Well, with all these holidays coming up, I just thought it might be fun to promote some bake sales.
>
> **YOU** (LEADER)
> That's interesting. But we should probably skip Halloween, since there wouldn't be enough time to prepare.
>
> **JAMES** (CO-WORKER)
> That makes sense. But Thanksgiving and Christmas could work.
>
> **YOU** (LEADER)
> My concern is that the first few months in any new hire situation are all about adapting to the job itself. Obviously, we want to build team cohesion and demonstrate our cultural values, but I'm not sure we've got the bandwidth to introduce something this drastic in the middle of Q4, especially since

the holidays themselves bring so many distractions on their own.

JAMES (CO-WORKER)
[disappointed] I realize all that, but I still feel like doing some non-work activities will help bring these new contributors up to speed more quickly.

YOU (LEADER)
I don't disagree at all that this is a good idea. I just think that it's a *lot* of change during a period when we don't have a ton of time to dedicate to making those changes. We'll have to plan for the invites, create the messaging, partner with the charities, set up the space for the sale, get the word out to the public... The list goes on. [cheerfully] Again, I love the idea. What if we have the cultural committee put out feelers on this and then circle back to it for Q1? January and February are always boring anyway. A bake sale would lift everyone's spirits. We'll have a new crop of hires by then, and they can be our guinea pigs.

JAMES (CO-WORKER)
[poker faced] I'll mention it at the next committee meeting.

The Win with a High-S (stabilizer)

» The High-S doesn't want to upset anyone, so he won't show much emotion. Don't be surprised if you get a little bit of a poker face. You might even wonder whether the message really resonated. But don't worry; the High-S profile just has to process and mull over the conversation a few times.

» Plan to circle back with him in a few days. Not tomorrow, but in a few days—after he has had ample time to think.

THE PROFILES

D (DRIVER)

How to Approach a High-D

» A High-D usually sees above the fray and focuses on the next exciting big thing. So it's important to remember that this bad idea of his could have just been something that came off the top of his head in the moment. He usually has no problem making suggestions before completely thinking them through.
» Either way, just let him talk. Don't get too judgmental. Drivers sometimes think out loud simply because their minds move too quickly otherwise.
» They're not going to get into the details. In fact, they're probably going to give you a few details with a lot of holes in them.
» Remember that he is trying to grow, move, excel, and conquer. He's going to think grand and big, and he won't spend much time wondering *how* we're going to do this.
» Don't beat around the bush. Don't be afraid to say no, because the Driver can take it. If you're the Driver's leader, however, you'll need to tell him more than just the *what*. Also tell him the *why*.

How to Pitch a High-D

» Use the Driver's underpinning fears that this idea will take a long time, be costly, or that the company will be taken advantage of.
» Make him aware that if we do this, we're going to have to do lots of detailed work and focus on a ton of minutiae for very little ROI. "The investment in time and energy is going to be significant," you might say. And you also might say, "The competition will be moving faster than what this is worth."

» You can argue the logic and facts of all of this, of course, but to truly change the High-D's mind, the thrust of the conversation has to play on his concerns.

The Win with a High-D

» A High-D will say "whatever" and just move on. He can take a no.
» That said, he might try to find another way to make it happen. Drivers are often entrepreneurs. They don't mind the fight. So don't be surprised if they come back with another angle or a different idea. That's fine. The flow of ideas is good for an organization.

(INFLUENCER)

How to Approach a High-I

» The High-I is naturally a salesperson, so prepare yourself for a great story. It'll be full of details and well articulated too. She will try to convince you by using emotion, stories, and anecdotes. She might even base the entire idea on one instance rather than a pattern. So don't be surprised if there's no research to back up the idea.
» The idea might appear a little self serving at first, because most likely, the Influencer is out to make the company and herself look good.
» You can tell the Influencer no, but be sensitive. Keep your message optimistic. Be sure to thank her for the idea and tell her how great it is, even if you don't intend to pursue it.

How to Pitch a High-I

» An Influencer's fears are always the same: This idea is going to embarrass her and/or the company. Changing her mind is a matter of making it clear that this will not make us look good. ("This is not the image we want to project." "This is not what

we want to be known for." "If we go down this route, people might think unfavorably of us.")
» The Influencer is always in favor of protecting the company's image. So focus on how a different decision could help us get better. ("We don't want to look like the flavor of the month and then have egg on our face when it's not relevant anymore.")

The Win with a High-I

» As long as you complimented the High-I and acted as her advocate, this conversation should be over.
» If she really believes in this idea and wants to put up a fight, then she will probably have a story about how it will work. It'll be an emotional and dramatic appeal. But ultimately, because she wants to be friendly and liked, she will probably accept your advice and move on.

 **(CONSCIENTIOUS)**

How to Approach a High-C

» This is the trickiest profile to dissuade. High-C's like Debora pride themselves on being thorough and analytical. Telling them that something isn't going to work is a tough one.
» The High-C will sound absolutely sure that this should happen. She has proof. Evidence. Logic.
» Expect to meet with tons of research. Does this mean she knows everything? Of course not. No one can. That is an area that you can use to your advantage.
» It's okay to get straight to the point with the Conscientious. You don't have to beat around the bush. But do spend time on the why and not just the *what*. The High-C needs explanations, and they'd better be steeped in data or you're going to meet with resistance.

How to Pitch a High-C

- » What the High-C fears most is being wrong or making a mistake.
- » When you pitch the Conscientious your opinion about her idea, her default assumption is going to be that you're saying she is wrong, even if you never expressly say "you're wrong." Never, ever use those words with a High-C, because to her, them's fightin' words.
- » To successfully dissuade a High-C, ask her to investigate things further. If you know a few facts that prove how bad an idea this is, then it's always a better play to let the High-C find those facts on her own. Her own analysis and research will be more effective at persuading her than you will be by telling her she's wrong.

The Win with a High-C

- » The High-C probably won't agree with you in some cases. But if you've provided enough logical, statistical analysis, you may have dissuaded her.
- » Conversely, if you don't have that data right at your fingertips and you've asked the Conscientious profile to research it on her own, it's a good plan to follow up in a day or two.
- » The High-C might be more willing to look into things and be open to investigation, but she probably isn't going to say, "You were absolutely right. What was I thinking?"
- » The Win is convincing the High-C to plug your variables into her equation for more consideration. She won't thank you, pat you on the back, and take you out to dinner. But if you're right and her research proves it, she will eventually let go of the idea.

DREADED CONVERSATION #7

I HAVE TO DELIVER BAD NEWS. HOW DO I DO IT?

Here we are in our final conversation. Now that you have had plenty of opportunity to practice identifying profiles and learning how to speak more effectively with them, we're going to do something a little different with this chapter: we're going to start by looking at *you*. As we engage the Approach to this conversation, we'll turn the examination inward and think about the best way to Approach someone with bad news based on *your* profile. From there, we will apply the best Pitch and the expected Win for each profile to whom you will deliver the bad news.

Let's get started.

As a leader or executive, you sometimes face situations where you have to deliver news that the recipient might consider bad. Maybe you have to fire someone.[1] Maybe you have to go negative on a performance review; or tell a customer something they won't like hearing; or change a relationship with a vendor; or tell an employee that promotion he was hoping for will be going to someone else. The

---

[1] The lessons in this chapter are certainly useful in situations where you have to fire someone, but they aren't by any means the handbook on the subject. If you work for an established company, chances are you already have a handbook for that—or at least there are well-established procedural guidelines to follow when you need to let someone go. If you do have these guidelines at your company, absolutely follow them. While you're following them, be mindful of the lessons in this chapter and the process will only become smoother and more positive for everyone involved.

list, of course, goes on. And while this is the last of our Dreaded Conversations, it's also the one I'm asked about most in my coaching sessions with leaders.

First, let's think about that problematic word "bad" in "bad news." If you think about this conversation as delivering *bad* news, then you're already putting yourself into the wrong frame of mind before you even start. Yes, this task is challenging. And, yes, it's uncomfortable. But if you approach it with a different mindset, then *challenging* and *uncomfortable* is all they will ever be. In other words, you have no reason to fear, or to feel that overwhelming sense of guilt that so many associate with these types of messages.

So, what is this different mindset toward delivering bad news? You need to remember that very encounter and conversation is an opportunity for growth and progress. It's a chance to help others get better. Even if you have to tell them something they won't completely love hearing, if you do it right, then they (and you) will benefit from the knowledge of how they can improve, grow, and behave in the way you're expecting.

Think of it this way: the situation that led to this conversation could be either **intrinsic** or **instrumental**. *Intrinsic* means that the situation is naturally bad in and of itself. Very little news is intrinsically bad. *Instrumental*, meanwhile, means that the value of the news—whether it's good or bad—is determined simply by how it is used. For example, is a candlestick good or bad? The answer is that it's neither. A candlestick has no intrinsic value. However, *how this candlestick is used* will determine if it's good or bad. If I take this candlestick and use it to hold a candle that will light a dark room when the power goes out, then the candlestick is good. But if I take that candlestick and, like in the game/movie *Clue*, I bash someone in the head with it, then the candlestick is bad.

So, there is no bad news or good news. It is only news. The question is what you do with it and how you deliver it. It's not a conflict or resentment conversation. It's a conversation about how to grow and get better.

If you do it right, you can transform every "bad news" situation into a helpful encounter that makes the recipient feel comfortable about how to improve their performance so this conversation doesn't ever have to happen again. To do this, we're going to transition away from "letting them down gently" and move toward "showing them that you care and want to coach them to become better at what they do." Do this and we increase their performance, not their resentment; we introduce corrections without crushing anyone's soul.

THE CONVERSATION

PARTICIPANTS

- » **SAM**, the owner of a rapidly growing clothing retailer
- » **CAITLIN**, a vendor, who has built her grassroots line of designer children's clothing with a tremendous amount of flash and pizzazz

LOCATION

- » The loading dock, while Caitlin (vendor) oversees the unloading of her summer line of sundresses and graphic T-shirts
- » There's quite a bit of noise, and plenty of people moving around at their various tasks while potentially watching the conversation unfold.

SAM (LEADER)
Caitlin, good. You're here. I've got something I need to—

CAITLIN (VENDOR)
[cutting in] Oh, hey, Sam, listen. I'm sorry we're late, but I worked all weekend to complete my new fall lineup. Today, I come bearing your monthly inventory and a taste of what's to come! You are the first person I'm showing these to, and I have to say – these – pieces – look – fabulous!

SAM (LEADER)
[clearly uninterested in the story] Look, Caitlin. We've hit a wall on your line's quarterly numbers. We're going to have to pass on all of it for now.

CAITLIN (VENDOR)

[wide-eyed] What are you talking about? Is this because I was late? I was working my fingers to the bone for days to complete this beautiful showcase for you. Look at all of this. You're going to pass on these masterpieces because I was late?

SAM (LEADER)

[commanding] No. I'm passing because your line's underperforming compared to others in stock.

CAITLIN (VENDOR)

[visibly shaken] Oh, come on. Everyone loves my clothes. People tell me all the time how creative and eye-catching my pieces are compared to what's normally in the stores. And you told me that you were all in for the next six quarters.

SAM (LEADER)

That was before I reviewed the numbers. I also told you a while back to create pieces that would appeal to a broader audience.

CAITLIN (VENDOR)

[pleading] I don't understand. How much social media *growth* have my designs created for your company? The shares and likes on your page have skyrocketed!

SAM (LEADER)

[frustrated] This doesn't have to be difficult. Yes, the social media stuff is encouraging. But the actual sales numbers are not. I appreciate the visibility, but what we need right now is to move product.

CAITLIN (VENDOR)

[looking around] You're going to be sorry about this. Your customers are going to be upset that you stopped carrying my lines. My work is loved and admired and appreciated by this community. You watch! Word will get out that you kicked me to the curb, and everyone will know the type of person you are! Your numbers will really go down the drain.

SAM (LEADER)

[turning to leave] Trust me, everyone will be saying, "It's about time I kicked that hippie's clothes out of the store. Get your clothing racks and boxes out of here. I've got other trucks coming in!"

THE ANALYSIS

SAM IS A HIGH-D (DRIVER)

Here is how we know:

» He demonstrated a tendency to be commanding and curt.
» He showed no interest in hearing any stories, explanations, or evidence.
» He was more interested in the numbers and results than in preserving the relationship.
» His short fuse got the better of him and resulted in a low blow to Caitlin as the parting shot.

DREADED CONVERSATION #7

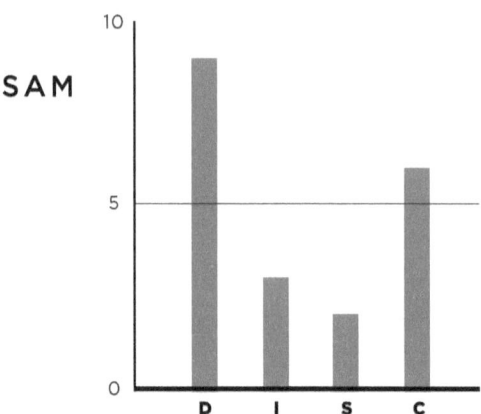

CAITLIN IS A HIGH-I (INFLUENCER)

» She was eager to tell a story about why she was late.
» She used the word "I" quite often, particularly in reference to her work.
» Her company's image is clearly important to her, as is the question of how the community will perceive her.
» Her actions, behaviors, and word choice were overly dramatic.
» There is no question that she was embarrassed by Sam's dismissal of her efforts.

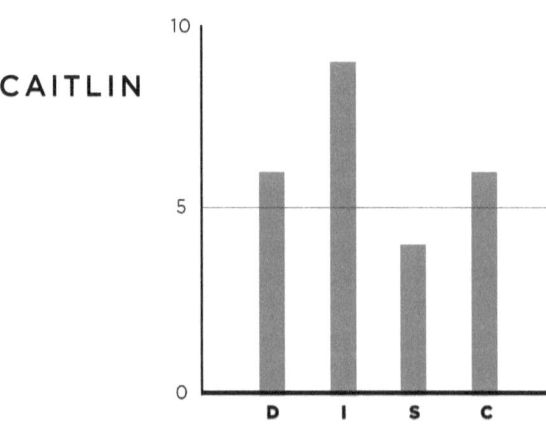

PERFORMANCE PRINCIPLE

Bandages and Sandwiches

People who have to deliver "bad" news tend to fall back on one of four typical approaches. So before we get into the *right* way to do this, let's look at a few *wrong* ways.

1. RIP OFF THE BAND-AID

High-D's and High-C's tend to favor this approach. They're naturally not as concerned about other people's feelings, and they're also much more results-oriented and driven by a desire to make progress. So they're often going to turn to strategies that get things done, even if it's at the expense of other people's feelings.

2. EASE OFF THE BAND-AID

High-I's and High-S's are exactly the opposite. They value other people's feelings over the desire to just get it over with. Where High-D's and High-C's want to rip off the Band-Aid, Influencers and Stabilizers are going to want to make sure we've run the bandage under some warm water for a few minutes, we have a cold compress ready, and that you've taken some Tylenol beforehand.

3. THE CRAP SANDWICH

This is a common (and much overused) strategy where you tell the recipient some good news at the start of the conversation, then after the person is buttered up, you deliver the bad news, and then immediately afterward, you finish with some more good news. So you're sandwiching the *crap* with some things that might make the recipient feel good. Theoretically, this is supposed to help soften the blow.

Theoretically...

The problem with the Crap Sandwich is that if you use it too often, the people around you will eventually pick up on your preferred method of delivering "bad" news and see right through it. In fact, they will start *anticipating* the pattern. In this case, two things happen: 1) they quit listening to the good news you deliver up front because they're just waiting for the hammer to drop with the bad news, and 2) they start expecting the hammer to drop in *all* cases where you pay them a compliment, even when you're not even planning on delivering bad news. Both can be particularly damaging to morale and productivity.

4. WAIT UNTIL THE END OF THE DAY

This is such a jerk move. Yes, waiting until the end of the day means that you can deliver the "bad" news then duck out for the sweet embrace of home, where you won't have to really face the problem. But it also robs the recipient of the opportunity to ponder what you've told them, think of follow-up questions to ask, and really find that chance to grow. The better play is to deliver the news early in the day, so that if they need to talk to you after they've had a chance to think, they have that opportunity.

BONUS CALL-OUT

The Talk, the Fix, and the Feelings

Based on research, case studies and my own client experiences, the most effective way to deliver *bad* news involves the perfect mix between ripping off the Band-Aid without warning and making sure the person is comfortable and encouraged throughout the process.

The bottom line is that you want to be direct and honest with people. No Crap Sandwiches and no dumping it on them at the end of the day. Tell them the news, but do it in a way that will engender hope and present an encouraging opportunity to improve. In other words, don't sugarcoat it. We don't want to treat them like a child. This isn't story-time. We shouldn't hem and haw. Just get it over with.

That said, your delivery should include three key components: the Talk, the Fix, and the Feelings.

1. THE TALK

Here's where you deliver the nuts and bolts of the message. The goal is to avoid mincing words, beating around the bush, and so on. Address the problem in a quick and straightforward way. Don't cause unnecessary anxiety by telling stories or prolonging the inevitable. Just deliver the news, highlight the problem, and move to the next step.

2. THE FIX

We're not just having a conversation about what is *wrong*. We're also going to talk about what needs to happen from now on. We're moving away from being just a bearer of bad news and toward becoming a helper and fixer.

Keep in mind that some people will feel defensive. This defensiveness might make them less open than usual about learning how to improve or correct an error. There will be some measure of resentment no matter what you do. So don't go in hoping to decrease the resentment; rather, find ways to move through the defensiveness so you can help increase future performance.

3. THE FEELINGS

I owe this method to Michelle Gielan, who, just like me, used to be in broadcast media for a national network before deciding to go into coaching and development. A graduate of the University of Pennsylvania, Michelle teaches this threefold approach to encouragement:

» First, paint an optimistic future.
» Second, play up the person's strengths.
» Third, point out some role models they can look to emulate as they adapt to the outcomes we're hoping to achieve.

The optimistic future can't be pie-in-the-sky thinking. We have to steep the encouragement in reality. Also, it must resonate with the other person by being a pursuit that they actually *want* and *need* to achieve.

In playing up the person's strengths, you're looking to point out the qualities they possess that will best help them progress toward the optimistic future. Tell them what's already working, what's right, and what's good. When you're done, they should have a clear sense of the tools in their toolbox that will help them get where they need to go.

Regarding role models, choose people who have achieved that optimistic future already. These people will model what the recipient needs to do to correct the situation.

THE APPROACH

As I mentioned in the introduction, we're going to do something a little different with this chapter. Instead of resolving our sample conversation first, we're going to arrange our discussion along the lines of the Approach, the Pitch, and the Win. Why? Because effectively Approaching each profile requires you to examine *your* profile first. If you're aware of your own tendencies when approaching this conversation, you can be effective with anyone, no matter what their profile happens to be.

IF YOU'RE A HIGH-D (DRIVER)

» Not everybody has your resiliency. To you, challenging news is just challenging news. When you get knocked down, you get right back up and fix the problem. But to anyone who isn't a Driver, this won't look like a problem that can be addressed quickly and easily.
» Certain tendencies of yours might lead the recipient to perceive you as insensitive. This is probably not true, of course. You might actually be quite sensitive, deep down. But that's not how the recipient is likely to view you.
» So, try to lead with sensitivity. You don't have to become a hypersensitive person, but do try to turn the sensitivity level up

a notch or two. Soften up your voice a bit, put some compassion in your eyes. This doesn't mean you're putting yourself in a weakened state. Rather, it means you're returning yourself to levels of sensitivity similar to those displayed by the other performance profiles.

If you're a High-I (influencer)

- » This is going to be difficult. Don't tell stories up front, try to buddy up, wander through different subjects, and avoid the true purpose of the conversation. Just get to the point.
- » Try not to worry about how this will make the recipient feel about you. It's difficult to feel like someone doesn't like you, but that will be the case here (if only for a little while).
- » Remember this key point to help you achieve the above: You're not delivering *bad* news; you're delivering an opportunity for the recipient to triumph in the future.

If you're a High-S (stabilizer)

- » Those points for the High-I apply to you, as well. Do your best not to avoid this situation.

If you're a High-C (conscientious)

- » Like the Driver, the challenge for you is that you will need to find a way to keep the recipient's *emotions* in mind. Most people aren't as logical as you want them to be. In fact, most people are much more emotional.
- » Avoid that tendency to focus solely on the realistic, bureaucratic approach and always trying to make the appeal strictly intellectual or logical. Yes, you might have all the data and all the answers and all the logic on your side, but your delivery can't be devoid of emotion. Bring some empathy, compassion, and understanding with you to the meeting.

THE PROFILES

 **(DRIVER)**

Now that we have thought about your Approach, we can turn our attention to the Pitch and Win for your *recipient's* profile.

To do this, we'll harken back to our three-pronged Pitch of *the Talk*, *the Fix*, and *the Feelings* for each profile. Nail these three elements and you'll be well on your way to achieving the Win, no matter what the news and no matter who you're talking to.

How to Pitch a High-D

» The Talk:
  › Get right to it. State the problem, then spend time focusing on *why* this situation is a problem.
  › High-D's tend to lack attention to detail because they focus on singular things (usually on whatever is top of mind). So we need to go further here. We need to make sure they understand *why* this is a real problem before we can move on to the Fix. Focusing on results and money will resonate best.

» The Fix:
  › Results-driven High-D's probably won't love that the Fix will take them some time to achieve.
  › Distract them from this notion by helping them visualize exactly how to grow toward the result.
  › Simplify the steps. Don't bog them down in twenty things that need to be changed. State the goal or result, then get out of their way.

» The Feelings:
  › High-D's might see encouragement as frivolous, extraneous stuff, but it *will* prevent them from stalling out on their path to the desired outcome.

> *Optimistic Future*: Talk to them about how/when they will succeed, achieve, conquer, and win.
> *Appeal to Strengths*: Point to a time in the past when they got knocked down and got back up quickly and succeeded. Play up their tenacity, resiliency, and tendency toward hard work.
> *Role Model*: Reference somebody who *wins*. It doesn't have to be anyone famous or fancy. Ideally, the role model will be someone who also didn't like going through all these "slow and stupid" hoops, but is now a highly successful producer (either in terms of money or outcomes).

The Win with a High-D

» A High-D may express their dislike and frustration, but they will be ready to move on.
» The question is, will they take action consistently and follow through over time? Some follow up and reinforcement will be necessary.

(INFLUENCER)

How to Pitch a High-I

» The Talk:
> Don't sugarcoat it.
> High-I's have a way of dramatizing and embellishing stories and facts, so don't overstate or understate the problem. Let's just get to the facts.
> This person is going to want to talk about the problem and give a thousand examples of why it happened. So if this is the first time the Influencer is hearing about this problem, go ahead and let them share a few (note: I said a *few*) examples.
> However, if this has become a persistent problem, don't let the conversation turn into a debate or a long-winded explanation.

- » The Fix:
  - › Don't get lost in a story. Tell the recipient operationally, and from a business-oriented perspective, why this situation is so important.
  - › If you're going to tell a story or paint an elaborate picture (which this profile will appreciate), make sure it's focused on the future solution, not on the problem and stories from the past.
- » The Feelings:
  - › Here's where you *must* tell stories, motivate, and inspire. Given the High-I's tendency toward storytelling, the recipient will especially appreciate this portion of the conversation.
  - › *Optimistic Future*: Make this colorful and also specifically about the recipient. The High-I should be the hero of this story. ("*You* will achieve this. *You* will be successful. *You* will win.") Remind them, also, that inspiration comes out of moments of desperation. When people get knocked down and then get back up and succeed, that's inspiring. ("When you walk through this challenge and come out on the other end, can you imagine how much people will admire you?)
  - › *Appeal to Strengths*: The Influencer is naturally going to have the ability to motivate, work with people, communicate, and share a vision. Even if they weren't able to do it this time, there are plenty of examples where they've been able to do it in the past. Remind them that now is a time to think that way, as well.
  - › *Role Model*: Pick a role model who isn't just a local figure, but somebody who is perceived well publicly. They should be someone that people in the community/region/nation recognize easily. It helps if this role model is also an Influencer.

The Win with a High-I

- » The High-I may have some trouble with emotions at first. Their focus will be on the image and reputation aspect.

» They will, however, readily embrace the chance to pursue that Optimistic Future.

 **(STABILIZER)**

How to Pitch a High-S

- » The Talk:
  - › State the facts in a softer tone. Yelling at this profile will produce the opposite effect of what you want. Pitch from a point of concern and frustration rather than a tone of anger and hostility.
- » The Fix:
  - › Help the Stabilizer understand why/how this happened and why/how things need to change.
  - › They will likely want to talk about the people and process side, so focus on how it impacts other people and the flow of business.
- » The Feelings:
  - › A High-S will respond better to how "we'll succeed" than how "you'll succeed." They're usually more concerned about the team effort than individual success or failure.
  - › *Optimistic Future*: The Stabilizer doesn't have to be in the spotlight, but they do need to be helpful and team oriented. Let them know that, if they make this change, many other people will benefit because of what they did.
  - › *Appeal to Strengths*: The High-S has an extraordinary ability to understand others, work hard to see beyond the surface of an issue, and listen to other people's needs. They also have a tremendous ability to organize and create a system/process for how the change you're pushing for could work. Lean on these abilities and you will get greater buy-in.

> *Role Model*: Point to someone who didn't just succeed, but who is admired by others (not necessarily in terms of glory, but as someone perceived as a good person and team player/great helper).

The Win with a High-S

» The High-S, like the High-I, will be eager to improve.
» If you've made it clear that this is best for everyone involved, and you have laid out a process for improvement, they will diligently work toward the fix.

 **(CONSCIENTIOUS)**

How to Pitch a High-C

» The Talk:
  > Don't mince words. Attempts to butter up a High-C will be met with suspicion, if not resentment.
  > The biggest problem will be getting the C to recognize or accept the bad news. So focus on the *why*. High-C's are great at analysis and logic—more specifically, their *own* logic. They have a much more difficult time viewing the logic behind another's perception of a mistake if the target of that mistake is the High-C.
  > Go into this talk expecting the Conscientious to *not* agree with your feelings, facts, or conclusion. They will probably explain that "other people messed up, not me." If by chance they do accept your premise, then you're way ahead of the curve.
» The Fix:
  > DO NOT tell them the fix! Take a much subtler and more diplomatic approach. This profile doesn't like being told what to think or do. They often believe that their way would be superior or smarter than your way.

> So, instead, use their problem-solving strength to your advantage. This person likes to solve puzzles, so deliver the news as an accepted, forgone fact, but then ask the Conscientious what should be done to remedy the issue moving forward.
  > Give them time to analyze. Ask them to think about it for a day or two and get back to you with answers.
» The Feelings:
  > *Optimistic Future*: We all know that perfect doesn't exist, but the picture to paint here is one where everything works perfectly (or at least better than it's currently working) and meets the highest standards. It sets the bar. ("Your work speaks for itself," you might say, "But if we make this change, then in the future, everyone is going to see how right you were and how high the quality of your product is.") It's a future where precision, quality, and intellect have excelled.
  > If you need the Conscientious to improve people skills or leadership skills, then make it a competition. ("Let's see who among the engineering team will be the best at encouraging teammates over the next month.")
  > *Appeal to Strengths*: The High-C has the ability to analyze, problem solve, spot mistakes, call attention to detail, and ensure high quality. Lean on these innate talents as evidence of their ability to move ahead and propel themselves forward.
  > *Role Model*: Pick someone who is very intelligent, someone the High-C already admires, and/or someone that the High-C should aspire to become like. This person should be well respected and considered an expert.

THE WIN WITH A HIGH-C

» While it is quite challenging to convince a High-C that she is wrong, if you've managed it successfully, you will see her move toward the Optimistic Future. It might require more time and deliberation on her part, but she will put in the work to improve. Some follow up and reinforcement will be necessary, especially regarding the importance of this new trajectory.

As a final note about delivering challenging news, consider this: when you're done, the Win won't involve goose-bump-inducing inspiration. Rather, you will have ensured that the recipient understands your decision and knows the what, why, and how we're going to fix the situation.

Another important thing to remember is that just because you've offered somebody a solution, that doesn't necessarily mean they'll take it. The Win is that we've made it easier for the recipient to accept this news and start taking the steps necessary to pursue that optimistic future.

PART 3
BONUS CHAPTER

BONUS CHAPTER

BETTER THAN GREAT

So we've come all the way to the final chapter, and now I'm going to hit you with the least controversial thing I could possibly say: perfection is impossible. Nothing and no one is perfect, so expecting perfection in how you engage with these conversations, or the DISC model as a whole, will only set you up for disappointment.

I tell my coaching clients that we can't focus on being perfect or even *great*. You will never arrive at perfection, of course, but the surprising point is that you'll also never achieve universally accepted *greatness*.

Rather than seeking to become the perfect leader, focus more of your energy on simply becoming a *better* leader. *Better* is better than great. It ensures that you are never satisfied with your existing achievements, and that you always strive to achieve more. To that end, for this bonus chapter, let's examine a specific area that each profile could try to improve and get better at every day. In other words, let's check those blind spots that are hindering us on our path to becoming a better leader.

A quick note before we get started: sometimes even your *strengths* can become blind spots. For example, I'm acquainted with an engineer and a lawyer, both of whom have High-C profiles. On his lunchbreak one day, the engineer created a spreadsheet of everything he thought his wife was doing wrong at home. The lawyer, meanwhile, came home and basically deposed his kids about where they were on a Friday night.

Now, the engineer's attention to detail is useful in most situations. And the lawyer's skill in a deposition has likely aided in many cases for him and his firm. But how do you suppose the engineer's wife reacted to the spreadsheet? And how did the lawyer's kids feel about their impromptu deposition? Those strengths don't always need to be shown in every encounter. If you lean on them in every situation, then they can sometimes become blind spots.

BLIND SPOTS

The High-D (driver)

If you're a Driver, you probably don't like getting caught up in the details, so every now and then, spend a little extra time focusing on the details.

Also, watch your tendency to come across as mean, insensitive, or aggressive. These qualities are really valuable for conquering and winning, but not as valuable when you need to connect with someone. That win-at-all-costs mentality probably won't help as much.

Work on being more caring. Start by asking people questions. Ask them how they feel. Ask them what they think. Seek consensus from the people you count on. Even if you don't genuinely care about this feedback, it's a "fake it till you make it" scenario.

When you communicate with people, try to be as specific as possible. Many High-D's will wonder why one of their employees delivered something that looks entirely different from what they were expecting. "Why did you do it this way?" the D will say.

"Well..." the employee will say. "Because you told me to."

"But that's not what I meant!" is the usual response from the D.

So be extremely cautious with your communication when you're giving directions and missions. And overall, work on getting better at communication and sensitivity.

The High-I (Influencer)

The first piece of advice here might seem a little odd, given what a tremendous speaker you are as a High-I, but it's this: work on becoming a better conversationalist. No, you don't need to learn how to talk more. Instead you need to start talking more about *others*. Start asking people about their interests. Make *them* the hero. You've never had a problem speaking about yourself (I should know, as I'm a High-I, and I used to be just like that). Do what I did: tweak your conversation so it's more others-focused whenever you can.

The second piece of advice might seem to run counter to the first, but hear me out: focus on speaking *less*. I can recall numerous times growing up, and even in my early career, when I would monopolize a conversation (because I'm such a *great* speaker and I had so many *great* things to say and don't you want to hear how *great* I am?). That was my mindset. As you might imagine, this can grate on some people. The simplest fix is to hear yourself doing it, and then change the subject to speak about the person with whom you're conversing.

It takes a lot of awareness to understand when you need to tone it down a little bit and become more others-oriented in your communication. But with practice, you'll start talking less, have shorter conversations and explanations, and spend less time talking about yourself and more time talking about others. You'll maintain all those great qualities that make you you, but you'll also start cutting down on this blind spot.

The High-S (Stabilizer)

For you, the High-S, it all starts with taking more action. Be more assertive. There's an old phrase that goes, "I'd rather ask for forgiveness than permission." This is a good mantra for the Stabilizer. Don't be so cautious. Don't wait. Don't worry so much about what other people will think. Make things move!

At the same time, you need to focus on being more direct with what you want, with what outcomes you're seeking, and about why we're talking in the first place. Also, there's no need to go into every gritty detail. We don't need to hear the whole thing. Give me a snapshot in a sentence or two and let's get to work.

High-S's tend to be long-winded, not because they're self-promoting or windbags, but because they're thorough and want to explain the whole process. But we don't always need that. Start with the outcome at the beginning of the talk, tell the recipient what you're going to tell them, and then tell them only the information they need to know. At the end, tell them what you just told them and give them some specific action. Be assertive. Come up with more actionable ideas instead of just information and details.

Finally, don't be afraid of conflict. You already know this is a problem, but now's the time to make a change. Conflict is inevitable. The mere fact that you don't like conflict could invariably cause conflict with other people. They'll be upset about why you're not taking action, or why you're avoiding them or hiding things from them. Recognize that the goal isn't to go through life without conflict; rather, it's to handle conflict well when it happens and then use it to get better.

The High-C (Conscientious)

High-C's, your blind spots are almost all about emotion. You've got the logic. You've got the knowledge. You've got the precision and attention to detail. Now it's time to bring the emotion to the table. I know it's tough because we put so much emphasis on what's right and what can be proven with our intellect. But that's not how most of the world operates. Most of the world is both logical *and* emotional.

Avoiding emotion might seem like a righteous path, but remember, we're checking our blind spots in this bonus chapter. We're trying to relate better to other people. This starts with making an honest effort to add more empathy, sympathy, and compassion into your conversations with people.

Next, stop trying to always be right. Your job isn't to right every wrong, because that's simply impossible in a world where "right" is oftentimes relative. Only a handful of things are *right* in the most absolute sense. If you want to get into the spiritual realm, the absolute rights are "thou shalt not murder," "thou shalt not steal," "thou shalt not lie," and so on. But even if you've done a year's worth of research that proves in your mind that Ford is always better than Chevy, that doesn't make it an absolute right. It means you've managed to rationalize your subjective opinion.

Self-righteousness never goes over well. So, admit to your mistakes when they happen. Humble yourself more often. That's even harder to do than it is to say, but if you start showing more sympathy and understanding for other people's opinions, then you'll connect with more people and have more effective conversations. Everything you do will be better.

FIGHTING THE GOOD FIGHT

Think about the arguments you have with the people you care about most. Parents. Spouse. Kids. Friends. Coworkers. If we ignore the specific content or purpose of those arguments, chances are that most of those fights are the result of the blinds spots in your profile that you've refused to check.

If you're a Driver and your mother is upset with you, it's probably not because of what you said, but rather, because you can sometimes seem uncaring and unsympathetic to her needs. If you're a High-C, maybe your spouse doesn't like that you come across so blunt and self-righteous. If you're an Influencer or Stabilizer, your kids maybe don't like that you feel the need to explain everything for fifteen minutes instead of just giving them a yes or no.

These are all things that would make anyone upset. The scenarios change, but the default behaviors of each profile do *not* change. It's up to you to check your blind spots, improve your communication, adapt your default, and make matters easier on everyone. It sounds tough, but you can do it. And when you do, everything will get easier, and all your relationships, both at work and at home, will improve. It won't be perfect, it won't make you great, but the effort will make each of these dreaded conversations be *better* than great.

WHAT'S NEXT?

If you found this book helpful, I'm delighted. However, learning DISC and how to tackle these dreaded conversations is only the beginning. It's just one piece of the performance-and-culture-improvement pie—other challenges like lack of teamwork, turnover, ineffective leadership and poor communication must be considered.

My organization shows people just like you how to apply the science, use my Performance Principles and psychology, and develop skills to achieve better performance. In other words, we show you how to get inside the minds of others to inspire productivity and a positive culture. Just like my client who testifies that his company has tripled its revenue and increased its size by 40% since we began working with them, (go look on page 5!), you too can see growth within your own organization with my help.

If you are looking to grow yourself, others, and your company, my team and I can help. Please visit us at **www.chrisflickinger.com**.

Oh! If you would like a little peek at some of the other performance science we provide our clients, you can follow me on social media **@itschrisflickinger** on the following platforms:

www.ingramcontent.com/pod-product-compliance
Lightning Source LLC
Chambersburg PA
CBHW031115080526
44587CB00011B/988